THE

QUARTERLY

EDITED BY

GORDON LISH

Sister Corrin had been warned not to let the flame-haired boy into her choir. I had a tie tied up tight against my throat and this glass-cracking voice Man, I wanted to sing! Mrs. Kellet kept warning that slender nun off. I sat in the front by choice after that, something a mischief sniffing kid like me would never have done. I sat there in the front in music class and blasted that soprano right into the gut of my bad rep. Sister Corrin could not keep still in her white fatigues, could not bear to hear this sweet bird out there and not throw her white shawl around him, not add this voice to the heavenly lift that went on behind the altar on Sundays. After six weeks of this, Sister Corrin could bear no more—and kept me in after class. I vowed. She smiled. This was in the fourth grade. I lasted five glorious weeks before I got the boot, before I was reclaimed by my seat mixed up with the bad boys in the back of that room. But I want you to know that there was a time in my life when I floated out over the front of an altar in my altar-boy smock—and that I have had a hard-on ever since.

—JOHN RYBICKI

N I N A   R O S E N W A L D : *Secret Agent*

THE
QUARTERLY

22 / SUMMER 1992

VINTAGE BOOKS

A DIVISION OF RANDOM HOUSE, INC.

NEW YORK

THE QUARTERLY (ISSN: 0893-3103) IS EDITED BY GORDON LISH
AND IS PUBLISHED MARCH, JUNE, SEPTEMBER, AND DECEMBER AT
201 EAST 50TH STREET, NEW YORK, NY 10022. SUBSCRIPTIONS—
FOUR ISSUES AT $48 US, $60 CANADIAN, $54 US OVERSEAS—AND ADDRESS
CHANGES SHOULD BE SENT TO THE ATTENTION OF SUBSCRIPTION OFFICE,
28TH FLOOR. ORDERS RECEIVED BY JANUARY 31 START WITH MARCH NUMBER;
BY APRIL 30, JUNE NUMBER; BY JULY 31, SEPTEMBER NUMBER; BY OCTOBER 31,
DECEMBER NUMBER. SEE LAST PAGE FOR PURCHASE OF BACK NUMBERS.

MANAGEMENT BY ELLEN F. TORRON
COORDINATION BY GEORGE DONAHUE
DESIGN BY ANDREW ROBERTS
ART DIRECTION BY CATHRYN AISON AND REBECCA AIDLIN
ASSISTANCE BY RICK WHITAKER AND NEAL DURANDO
PUBLICITY BY V. G. DAWSON

THE QUARTERLY WELCOMES THE OPPORTUNITY TO READ WORK OF EVERY
CHARACTER, AND IS ESPECIALLY CONCERNED TO KEEP ITSELF AN OPEN FORUM.
MANUSCRIPTS MUST BE ACCOMPANIED BY THE CUSTOMARY RETURN MATERIALS,
AND SHOULD BE ADDRESSED TO THE EDITOR. *THE QUARTERLY* MAKES THE UTMOST
EFFORT TO OFFER ITS RESPONSE TO MANUSCRIPTS NO LATER THAN ONE WEEK
SUBSEQUENT TO RECEIPT. OPINIONS EXPRESSED HEREIN ARE NOT NECESSARILY
THOSE OF THE EDITOR OR OF THE PUBLISHER.

COVER BY CHIP KIDD

ISBN: 0-679-74050-3

YOU PROBABLY SHOULD BE TOLD MARELLO'S NOVEL IS NOT APPEARING HERE
EXACTLY IN THE CONDITION OF COMPLETION THAT SHE DELIVERED IT TO US IN.
THE THING IS, WE HAD TO GO FORCE IT INTO OUR FORMAT. THAT'S ONE
THING. THE OTHER THING IS THIS—WE KNOCKED OUT SOME ELEMENTS
OF IT IN ORDER TO CREATE ROOM FOR SOME ITEMS WE FIGURED WE
JUST HAD TO CREATE ROOM FOR. IT'S WHAT HAPPENS WHEN ROOM-MAKING
IS THE BUSINESS YOU DECIDE YOU'RE IN. WELL, YOU MIGHT SAY:
LOOK, FELLAS, COULDN'T YOU DO WITH ONE LESS PAGE OF HOGAN, FOR
GODDAMN INSTANCE? AND THE ANSWER WOULD BE: HELL, NO, WE COULDN'T.
WHICH WOULD SEEM PRETTY CRAZY AND NASTY ON THE FACE OF IT—TAKE
FROM MARELLO AND GIVE TO HOGAN. BUT THERE IT IS, CRAZY AND NASTY
IF THIS IS THE WAY YOU WANT TO SEE IT. HEY, ISN'T IT MARELLO HERSELF
WHO REPORTS TO US ON THE ROOM THE PAINTERS GOT THEIR HANDS
ON AND INTO WHICH SPACE THEY SOUGHT TO JAM EVERYTHING THEY FELT
COUNTED? IT JUST *ALL* HAD TO GO *IN*, YOU KNOW?
AND, PRESTO-AMAZO, IT SORT OF ALWAYS DOES.

THE QUARTERLY

22 / SUMMER 1992

NÔTRÈ PËNSÈES

SECOND, HARRIS

A NACE PAGE   2

LAURA MARELLO /
    The Tenants of the Hôtel Biron   *3*

PAUL CODY / *Hey to All My Family*   *203*

JASON SCHWARTZ / *Ox*   *204*

RICHARD BLANCHARD /
    Information   *208*

JOE KERR / *A Crucifixion*   *209*

ANOTHER NACE PAGE   *210*

ZERO HOPELÖFF   *211*

KEVIN GRIFFITH   *215*

BRUCE BOND   *218*

TIMOTHY LIU   *219*

ONE MORE NACE PAGE   *222*

PAULETTE JILES *to* Q   *223*

JOHN RYBICKI *to* Q   *226*

LYDIA DAVIS *to* Q   *227*

CYNTHIA OZICK *to* Q   *228*

PAULETTE JILES *to* Q   *229*

WAYNE HOGAN *to* Q   *232*

CAMPBELL GEESLIN *to* Q   *244*

THE LAST NACE PAGE   *247*

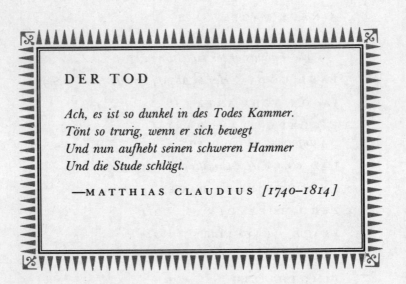

DER TOD

Ach, es ist so dunkel in des Todes Kammer.
Tönt so trurig, wenn er sich bewegt
Und nun aufhebt seinen schweren Hammer
Und die Stude schlägt.

—MATTHIAS CLAUDIUS *[1740–1814]*

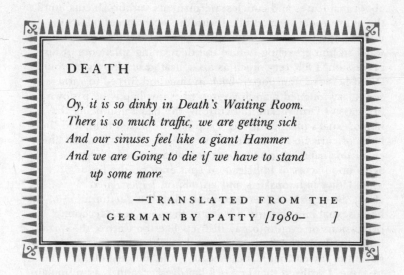

DEATH

Oy, it is so dinky in Death's Waiting Room.
There is so much traffic, we are getting sick
And our sinuses feel like a giant Hammer
And we are Going to die if we have to stand
    up some more.

—TRANSLATED FROM THE
GERMAN BY PATTY [1980–   ]

THE COST OF PRODUCING THESE PAGES IS MET BY INSTRUMENT OF A TWENTY-FIRST CENTURY "HANDS ACROSS THE WINE-DARK SEAS" OUTREACH PILOT GRANT (#2787-4-XX1.C) MOUNTED UNDER THE JOINT SPONSORSHIP OF THE INTER-LINGUAL UNION, THE E.J. CRACKEL PROJECT FOR WORLD MUTUALITY, AND TEEN 'N' TWENTY DRESSES OF RAHWAY, NEW JERSEY. *THE QUARTERLY* WISHES TO ACKNOWLEDGE ITS GRATITUDE TO THESE ORGANIZATIONS FOR THEIR EXPRESSION OF TRUST IN THIS PUBLICATION'S STEWARDSHIP. THANKS, TOO, TO THE TRANSLATO WHEEL CORPORATION.

Second, Harris

After rubbing ourselves together like two dry sticks in hopes of raising a few sparks to enkindle the tepid embraces of safe sex, a recent trick and I exchanged words, fluids being out of the question, as we settled down snugly on my squalid futon to tell each other our life stories—or, more specifically, *his* life story, for *I* listened while *he* talked, rhapsodizing about his glamorous career as a hairdresser and his boyfriend's as a make-up artist, about manicures and cuticles, permanents and brush cuts, until the entire room seemed filled with the sickly sweet odor of mousse and the acrid smoke of singed hair. Suddenly, as I watched him groveling before the demeaning splendors of his profession, I felt very much as an educated black person would feel if he were transported back in time and forced to witness some lazy-tongued mandingo describe how happy he is down on his massa's farm pickin' dat cotton—the hair salon being the homosexual's plantation, the scalp his sun-baked field, and the bales of curls he harvests the cash crop he reaps. Hearing him chant this happy spiritual about the pleasures of tilling acres upon acres of follicles and split ends on the heads of white ladies in hoopskirts and crinolines, I speculated about the degree of coercion involved in the ghettoization of the homosexual into the arty barrios of the so-called "accepting" professions or even into gay districts like the Castro, the quaint little shtetl where I live. As I permitted the unchecked stream of my partner's anesthetizing volubility to roll over me, I realized that he, as a hairdresser, and I, as an inmate of the neighborhood in which I am effectively interned, were victims of a colorless apartheid, an unspoken ultimatum that encourages the homosexual not only to tolerate but to embrace his oppression, allowing himself to be herded like cattle into residential ghettos and special subdivisions of the work force. With no underclass to shore up our credentials for persecution, it is almost impossible to recognize this nonracial Jim Crow as discrimination because it seems to occur with the full complicity of the discriminated party, who willingly shuffles to the back of the bus. But in the excited descriptions of grandeur by the bootlickers of the beauty and entertainment industry, I hear the crack of the foreman's whip lashing at the shoulders of millions of grinning Uncle Toms.

—DH

THE
QUARTERLY

LAURA MARELLO

The Tenants of the Hôtel Biron

A collection of monographs
by the tenants of the Hôtel Biron,

Originally written
for the magazine *Camera Work.*

Edited, with an introduction
by Geoffrey Hildebrand.

Translated by Slavita Jovan.

EDITOR'S INTRODUCTION

TRANSLATOR'S NOTE

ACKNOWLEDGMENTS

THE MANUSCRIPTS:

The Consolations of Erik Satie

The Histories by Pablo Picasso

Brief Lives by Henri Matisse

Letters Not Sent: The Letters
of Camille Claudel to Auguste Rodin

The Spiritual Exercises of Vaslav Nijinsky

The Notebooks of Eduard Steichen

THE TENANTS

The Hôtel Biron was originally one of the most luxurious mansions in the Faubourg St-Germain. It was designed in the eighteenth century by Jacques-Ange Gabriel, the architect of the Petit Trianon and the palaces on the Place de la Concorde in Paris. For a time it served as the Couvent du Sacré Coeur. After the nuns left, it was placed in the hands of M. Ménage, a liquidator of government property, who found the mansion in a state of disrepair. He left the mansion as it was, allowed the garden to grow wild, and rented the rooms to artists.

In 1907, Eduard Steichen, the young American photographer whom Rodin had called to his Meudon residence to photograph his Balzac by moonlight, rented a room upstairs. The Cubist painter Pablo Picasso also came to the Hôtel Biron in 1907 and brought with him the Douanier Henri Rousseau, that startling, ingenuous painter whom Picasso would honor at a party at the Bateau Lavoir. The Douanier's primitivism, his uncanny lack of perspective, the colorful, childlike portraits and surreal landscapes were the foundations for the new art of Picasso and his circle. "Rousseau is not an accident. He represents the perfection of a certain order of thought," the Spaniard had said at the raucous debauch in Rousseau's honor. Usually the butt of cruel jokes, Rousseau was touched by Picasso's friendship. Rousseau had lost his lodgings through a misunderstanding, so Picasso and Rousseau rented adjacent rooms at the Hôtel Biron. Picasso retained his studio at the Bateau Lavoir. Like many other artists of the time, Picasso would acquire several studios and residences.

Picasso continued his tradition of wild parties at the Hôtel Biron. According to one biographer, the tenants of the Hôtel Biron were finally evicted because of a baptismal party Picasso held in the nuns' former chapel and sacristy, where the Spaniard had built an elaborate Roman bath, tile lounging area, and fountains.

By 1907, the painter Henri Matisse had achieved notoriety. The painting classes he had started in his studio at the Couvent des Oiseaux had become so popular that Matisse was obliged to rent a larger studio at the Hôtel Biron to accommodate his increasing number of students. He also took rooms in the mansion.

In September of 1908, the German poet Rainer Maria Rilke moved into the upstairs rooms in the southeast corner of the Hôtel Biron, previously occupied by his wife, Clara Westoff, a sculptress and former student of Rodin's. In a letter to Rodin, Rilke urged the Master to move in, and likened the rabbits scampering through the overgrown garden outside to a scene in a Chinese tapestry.

At that time Rodin was living at the Villa des Brillants in Meudon with Rose, his life-long companion. Though he had many studios and residences in Paris, *pied-à-terres* and *garçonnières*, some known to friends and public, some secret, he was drawn to the huge estate at 77 rue de Varenne, in part because of Rilke's pleadings, in part because of the inherent lure of the place—its view, its wildness, its vast, untamed strength. Rodin said the place had a mischievous charm that intrigued him, and he took over the ground floor rooms on the southwest side, using them as studio space and staying there for weeks at a time, until Rose sent their son to the place with threats.

Once Rodin had settled there, he immediately installed his former mistress, Camille Claudel, a great sculptress in her own right and a former student of Rodin's, who, since their ten-year stormy affair ended in 1891, had slowly begun to withdraw into her studio.

Also in 1908, the avant-garde French writer Jean Cocteau, soon-to-be darling of the Ballets Russes, was wandering through the Faubourg St-Germain and stopped in to take a look at the Hôtel Biron. According to Cocteau's memoirs, the concierge showed him rooms that were available: the former dance and music classrooms of the nuns, accessible only by passing through the empty chapel. Cocteau made an offer to the liquidator that afternoon and kept the rooms until the artists were evicted after the war, at the end of 1918.

Erik Satie was the next to arrive. During his ten years of self-imposed exile in the suburbs, Satie had come to Paris only at night, carrying a hammer in his pocket. He earned his living playing piano in the Auberge du Clou or Le Chat Noir. Fiercely independent, he reemerged in 1910. He settled happily with the other tenants at the Hôtel Biron, in the room Rousseau vacated at his death.

The famous dancer of the Ballets Russes, Vaslav Nijinsky, was not long in seeking his lodgings at the Hôtel Biron. Soon after meeting Rodin in 1912, in the middle of his own *succès de scandale*, and against the wishes of the impresario and owner of the Ballets Russes, Sergei Diaghilev, Nijinsky was invited to Rodin's apartments. A year later he moved in upstairs, into the room which Camille Claudel had vacated.

COLLABORATION

It is difficult to understand how ten great artists, with such force of personality, such eccentricities and individualistic strains, and such opposing theories on art, could live under one roof with nothing in common except their artistic genius. But the Picasso-Satie-Cocteau collaborations for the Ballets Russes and their wild parties are well known. These great *soirées,* usually organized by Picasso, were vivid festivals, celebrations of talk, drink, and dance, and it was not long before *tout Paris* wanted an invitation to the affairs.

Rodin had attended the scandalous opening of *L'Après-midi d'un Faune* in 1912, where Nijinsky's performance was met with jeers and outrage. Backstage after the performance, Rodin met Nijinsky and Diaghilev. In 1916, Picasso and Matisse would sponsor the Granados-Satie concert, and in 1917, Picasso, Satie, and the Ballets Russes would perform Satie and

Cocteau's *Parade.* But there was another collaboration going on among the tenants of the Hôtel Biron, a collection of monographs written for *Camera Work*, which, though originally intended for publication, were never printed. It was these papers that I found, to my delight and revelation, when I was admitted into the basement archives of the Musée Rodin on that rainy afternoon in Paris twenty-three years ago in 1967.

Soon after Rodin's death in 1917, the French government locked the basement of the Hôtel Biron, where they had placed in storage all the letters, bills, papers, and documents relating to Rodin, together with many unexhibited drawings and plaster casts by the Master. In 1918, when the other tenants of the Hôtel Biron were evicted and the Hôtel became the official Musée Rodin, the basement archives were declared closed to scholars and art historians for fifty years after Rodin's death, in accordance with French canonical law. By the year 1967, when the archives were finally opened to scholars, few people remembered that the Musée Rodin was once the Hôtel Biron, where Rodin occupied the downstairs rooms and the upstairs was rented, flat by flat, by painters, poets, a photographer, a dancer, and a composer.

While the other scholars huddled around Rodin's widely publicized erotic drawings, mused over the remnants of uncast plasters, and inspected his elaborate filing system of letters, bills, and foundry receipts, I was drawn to a far corner of the basement where a clutter of disorganized manuscript pages lay strewn about the floor, tables, and shelves. I began to pick up and stack the pages, and in doing so, I found that though they were all inscribed *for Camera Work*, I could find at least six different styles of handwriting among the random pages.

I would spend the next few weeks in that corner of the basement, uncovering as many stray sheets of paper as I could find which bore the inscription *for Camera Work*, and sorting them according to penmanship, content, and style. I would spend the ensuing twenty years editing them.

The origins of this collection of monographs written by

the tenants of the Hôtel Biron for *Camera Work* are explained in Steichen's *Notebooks*. With the cooperation of Steichen, in 1905, the American photographer Alfred Stieglitz opened the 291 Gallery in New York. Beginning in 1908, with Steichen's assistance, Stieglitz exhibited work at the 291 Gallery by the tenants of the Hôtel Biron: Matisse, Picasso, and Rodin. Since 1902, Steichen and Stieglitz had also been collaborating on Stieglitz's quarterly, *Camera Work*. According to Steichen's *Notebooks*, in 1908, at the time of the Rodin and Matisse shows at the 291, Stieglitz asked Steichen to arrange for several monographs to be written by the tenants, to be published as a special edition of *Camera Work*.

In 1918, when the Hôtel Biron was reclaimed by the state for the Rodin Museum, these monographs were locked in the basement of the Hôtel Biron as part of the museum's archives. It is unclear why more care was not taken with the manuscripts. Apparently, the French officials moved the museum's belongings to the basement in great haste, in fear of the sycophants who would come to claim valuable busts, small plasters, and drawings as souvenirs. The tenants of the Hôtel Biron did not demand access to the basement to retrieve their manuscripts. According to Steichen's *Notebooks*, the tenants were afraid the government might confiscate their property and suppress the manuscripts.

Though Stieglitz ceased publication of *Camera Work* in 1917, the artists continued work on the monographs in hopes that Stieglitz would publish them in book form or in another quarterly. Stieglitz did produce a magazine called *MSS* from 1922 to 1925, but the tenants' monographs were never published. Stieglitz abandoned the project sometime between the two world wars, after the tenants of the Hôtel Biron had been evicted and Stieglitz's friendship with Steichen had cooled.

THE MANUSCRIPTS

Each artist created a monograph that is different from those of the other tenants, and peculiar to his or her own artistic temperament. Some of the works chronicle the artistic movements of the time, others celebrate life in Paris; some reflect life at the Hôtel Biron, others the personal musings of the tenants.

Picasso's *The Histories* describes the art movements of the period as if he were writing a mock-anthropological document. Matisse's *Brief Lives* paints psychological portraits of the Hôtel Biron tenants. Steichen's *Notebooks* is primarily concerned with daily life at the Hôtel Biron. *The Consolations* is Satie's bizarre record of life in Paris at the turn of the century and his advice on how to live there. In the *Letters Not Sent*, Camille Claudel expresses her desires, anger, and frustration, and chronicles her journey into poverty and despair. Nijinsky's *The Spiritual Exercises* uses Saint Ignatius Loyola's imaging method to understand feelings.

TRADITION AND PRECEDENT

Collective memoirs of this kind were not common at the beginning of the twentieth century, but the individual manuscripts all draw their forms from older, established works, and some are directly based on particular classics, so deliberately that they take their title from the older work.

The manuscripts by Matisse, Picasso, and Nijinsky fall into this latter category. Matisse's *Brief Lives* takes its title from John Aubrey's work of the same name. Vasari's *Lives of the Artists* is a similar work. It is interesting to note that Vasari, like Matisse, was a painter who chose to honor his fellow artists (including Michelangelo) by writing their biographies. Vasari, however, became better known for the *Lives* than for his painting, whereas Matisse is still known almost exclusively for his work in the visual arts.

Picasso's *The Histories* takes its title from the fifth-century B.C. work of the same name, written by the Greek historian Herodotus. Herodotus's style was rambling, as is Picasso's, his task gargantuan, and many of his tales, though stupefying and generally enlightening as to the culture or rituals of the people described, are inaccurate in their details. Picasso's *The Histories* captures the spirit and scope of the original.

Nijinsky's *The Spiritual Exercises* takes its name from the sixteenth-century work by Saint Ignatius Loyola. It uses the imaging method of that work and employs it in the understanding of feelings.

The manuscripts of Claudel and Steichen follow the standard forms of letters and notebooks. Claudel's *Letters* seems to owe something in content and style to *The Letters of a Portuguese Nun*, another found manuscript written in the seventeenth century by a nun to her lover, the Marquis de Chamilly, who promised to marry and subsequently abandoned her. Rilke was familiar with that work and had even translated it. According to Steichen's *Notebooks*, he showed it to Rodin. Perhaps Rilke, or even Rodin, showed it to Camille Claudel.

Steichen's *Notebooks* follows in the tradition of that form. The notebooks are somewhat similar to *Delacroix's Journal*, which was popular among artists at that time.

It is interesting to note that among his published writings, Satie had a work entitled *Memoirs d'un Amnésique*. Satie's *The Consolations* uses some of the ideas from the *Memoirs*.

THE EDITORIAL TASK

In editing the manuscripts, I have endeavoured to present the works as a whole, without the scholarly intrusions of footnotes, textual analysis, and marginalia. I have refrained from inserting any commentary into the text itself.

Geoffrey Hildebrand
April 26, 1990—San Francisco, California

LAURA MARELLO

TRANSLATOR'S NOTE

Under the diligent supervision of the editor, Geoffrey Hildebrand, I chose the team of translators who have rendered the English-language version of this manuscript, most of which was originally written in French, German, Spanish, and Russian. I worked in close consultation with the translators and was ultimately responsible for the final results.

In translating the works, my primary concern was to render as literal a translation as possible, in keeping with the innovative translation theories introduced by the Island School of Criticism. As to other matters, the overall vision for the book rests with the editor, and its success belongs to him.

The translators who worked on the manuscript are Riiki Westerschulte (German), Uriel Peña (Spanish), Juvenal Tomczak (Russian), and David Lapin (French).

Slavita Jovan
April 26, 1990—San Francisco, California

ACKNOWLEDGMENTS

Through the generosity of a grant by the Nevin Dyhogi Research Institute for Correspondences Among the Arts, it was possible to travel extensively in Europe and Russia, enabling us to visit the museums and archives necessary to authenticate the manuscripts. Leodegario Huerta, curator of the Picasso Museum in Barcelona, made his archives available to us in the best spirit of scholarship. Gottfried Hermann of the Rilke Library in Munich made available certain of the library's files and also proved a marvelous source of technical information. During our sojourn in Russia, we received helpful advice from Gunter Grodzitizki of the Moscow Ballet.

The entire project depended heavily on the cooperation

and expertise of Robert Periquet, Conservateur of the Musée Rodin in both Paris and Meudon. Without his talent, patience, and flexibility, the success of our venture would have been severely compromised. Also in Paris, for their invaluable biographical assistance, we are indebted to Dominique Villiaume of the Sorbonne, who provided us with documents from their Cocteau archive; Henri Courtois of the Collège de France, executor of the Claudel estate; and Geneviève Marceau of the Institut Musical Erik Satie.

At home in the United States, we would also like to acknowledge the kind cooperation of Peter Jupiter, executor of the Steichen estate. The realization of this project would hardly have been possible without his assistance. We thank Tom Hunger of the Island School of Criticism, who has taken much time away from his own research in order to work as a consultant on this project. We benefited particularly from the skillful assistance of Rudy Mabutas, the Rousseau expert at the Museum of Modern Art in New York, and Ottavio Melfi, their Matisse scholar.

In California, we give our special thanks to the gracious assistance of Edward Harpoothian, Rodin scholar and curator of the Cantor collection at Stanford, and to Ion Constantinescu, Director of the Palace of the Legion of Honor in San Francisco, where a wealth of Rodin bronzes, drawings, and documents are housed.

For their probing questions and sharing of discoveries, we thank our two sons, Valto and Sandro.

The final word of thanks must go from me alone to my wife, Slavita Jovan. Though the editorship bears my name only, Slavita traveled everywhere with me, acted as my translator in many countries, assisted tirelessly with all phases of the manuscript, and provided constant support and encouragement, without which I could never have finished. The realization of this vision owes to her.

Geoffrey Hildebrand
April 26, 1990—San Francisco, California

The Consolations of Erik Satie

CHOOSING THE PROPER CURE

Doctors are quacks, so it is important to choose the right one. Sometimes this can be done by selecting the proper cure for your ailment. The following cures are currently available, and these come with my opinions and commentary:

Travel, Change of Climate: This is said to cure moral diseases, profound sorrows, hallucinations, and monomania. It does not help nervousness. It cures obesity in lymphatics but not others. It cures disordered imaginations, unbridled passions, jealous characters, worried dispositions, and headaches, but only in thin women.

Taking the Waters: This does not cure anything, but it is satisfying if you wish to gamble or find your daughter a husband. Mont Doré, Cauterets, and Eaux Bonnes are said to specialize in sore throats. Saint-Sauver is said to specialize in neuralgia, hysteria, and hypochondria. Plombières specializes in other female disorders. Luchon and Aix-Les-Bains will not cure you of gambling. You may take the grape cure, milk cure, and whey cure anywhere, but you can only find the earth cure at Arcachon and Aix. It is supposed to be good for gout. The Law of 1893 excludes water cures from its free medical assistance, so if you want to gamble and find your daughter a husband, you have to pay your own way.

Chloroform, Ether and Alcoholism: These kill pain, are useful in reducing fever, and work well as tranquilizers. I do not recommend them in excess, except for the alcoholism.

Incarceration in an Insane Asylum: Cures old age, blackmail, unorthodoxy, and is very useful in getting rid of one's enemies. This is a very effective cure.

Invoking Saint Blaise, Patron Saint of Motorcyclists with Colds: I hear this is quite successful in curing a variety of ailments.

Throwing Yourself at the Mercy of Your Neighborhood Sorcerer: I recommend blacksmiths for problems with the devil, cobblers for problems with women. For other problems, you may consult midwives, undertakers, or children who want to be priests.

Drug Cures: Quinine is said to cure infectious diseases, colds, skin troubles, anemia, and neuralgia. Potassium iodide is prescribed for indigestion, high blood pressure, heart trouble, and obesity. Iron is good for paleness, breathlessness, stomach pains, anemia, neurasthenia, tuberculosis, kidney problems, and arthritis. Bicarbonate of soda is good for diabetes and bronchitis. Belladonna is recommended for eye problems and colds.

Resetting the Stomach: This is highly recommended if your stomach has been dislocated.

Retiring to the Country: This cures people who are suffering from excessive ambition. When you retire to the country, take long walks, hunt, eat light food, undergo massages and warm baths, and engage in varied reading. Humiliate your pride and raise obstacles against your desires. Acquire modest friends without aspirations.

Leeches: Put them in your bed at night, and if they latch on to you, feed them well and promise to marry them, but then at the last minute make some excuse.

Severe Diets: I approve of anything severe. Find a doctor who will put you on a series of severe diets, a different one each week. This is the perfect cure.

Breast Feeding: You can try this cure, but the woman may complain about your sordid rooms, and then you'll have to let her go.

Fresh Air, Exercise, Water Drinking, Vegetarianism: Hogwash. It makes you oversensitive, and you're bound to contract every ailment that's tangoing through Paris.

Camphor: It probably works, but think what it will do to your social calendar.

Deep Breathing and Spitting: It sounds vigorous and calisthenic to me. Try it once.

Vaccination: A tricky business at best.

Artificial Insemination: I don't know what it will cure, but it sounds like an interesting idea.

Living on a Boat in the Seine and Playing Music During Meals: It makes the fish terribly ill.

Electro-physiochemical Treatments: I hear they make you lose your appetite for cognac, and for this reason I cannot recommend them.

Bonesetting: I cannot recommend it, unless you've broken one.

Urine Healers: I cannot recommend them.

Being Tied Down to a Wooden Plank and Having Cold Water Thrown Over You: The Academy of Medicine opposes it. A friend can do it to another friend, as long as neither is a doctor.

HOPELESS CASES

If you're suffering from circular folly, dual folly, delirium of persecutions, hysteria, shoplifting, hallucinations, freewill, or insanity, there may be no help for you. On the other hand, now that the source of the emotions has been transferred from the stomach to the brain, the nervous intestinal system of insects is being studied, bifurcation is being disputed, and education has been recognized as a form of both suicide and homicide, maybe doctors can offer more hope.

ABOUT DOCTORS

If it's too perplexing to choose a cure, a simpler method might be to choose a doctor and let him choose the cure. But if you're going to choose a doctor, there are some things you should know and some recommendations I would like to make.

Dr. Broussais believes that all diseases are caused by inflammation of the intestines. I would recommend that painters see Dr. Broussais, since the only thing they do besides paint is complain of stomach ache.

If you want Dr. Ricord as your doctor, you must know

which room to wait in. If you're an ordinary person, meaning that you possess no memorable birthmarks and no money, you'll have to wait in a crowded room and be assigned a number. If you're a woman, you'll have to enter by a separate staircase and are advised to speak to no one. If you bring a letter of recommendation, you'll be seated in a separate room with others like you. If you're a friend of the doctor, or a doctor, or a doctor of the doctor, or a doctor's doctor, you'll be assigned to yet another room.

Another reason to visit Dr. Ricord is his collections. He has two Rubenses and a Van Dyck in the reception salon. He has a collection of busts of physicians in the library. In the same library, he has a collection of surgical instruments. When members of the aristocracy fight duels, they have been known to select Dr. Ricord's surgical instruments as weapons.

A reason not to visit Dr. Ricord is that he believes syphillis is not contagious.

If you stammer, Dr. Becquerel and Dr. Jourdan are your men. Don't try to choose between them. They often argue publicly over their cures, which of course contradict each other. I'm sure if you attend one of these disputes, this will cure your stammer.

Dr. Piorry invented a method called plessimetrism, which means tapping on your abdomen to find out what's wrong with your organs. It's a very musical idea, and I recommend a recreational visit.

I would avoid all doctors who practice Phrenology, Cranioscopy, Physiognomy, Microscopy, Magnetism, Numerology, Pharmacology, Chemistry, Cosmobiology, Acupuncture, Homeopathy, Humorology, Psychoanalysis, Hydrology, Thermology, Eclecticism, Pantheism, or Anglophilism.

If it's a miracle cure you want, Dr. Boissarie has been running an authentication bureau just for Lourdes and can tell you which ones are reliable.

You may want to throw up your hands and choose your doctor according to his hobby. All doctors have one. Dr. Herard plays the piano. Dr. Robin runs a metallurgical factory and reviews for *The New York Herald*. He was also a consultant to the Tsar of Russia. Dr. Brocq collects Impressionist paintings. Dr. Halle himself paints.

When visiting a doctor, make sure to haggle over the fee, and don't let him charge you more than ten francs. For dentistry, choose a dentist who began as a locksmith. They are the most sympathetic. Don't see any doctor who wears the *palmes academiques*; that's just a ruse to drive up prices. Doctors who require you to make an advance reservation are respectable, but you may get nervous if you know about your appointment too far ahead.

If the doctor you choose died a long time ago, which he invariably has, find out who the deceased's students were. Then choose the one who opposed the doctor's teaching and developed a theory and practice of his own.

SELF-DIAGNOSIS

If you prefer self-diagnosis and self-cure, I recommend the following reading: *The Natural History of Health and Illness*, F. V. Raspail, 1848; *Treatise on Venereal Diseases*, Phillipe Ricord, 1838; *The Moral Treatment of Madness*, Dr. Leuret, 1840; *Common Sense Medicine*, Dr. Piorry, 1868; *Manual of Health and Advice on the Art of Healing Oneself*, Dr. Jean Giraudeau de Saint Gervais. These books can be found in any grocery store.

PERSONAL REMEDIES

My personal cures are as follows:

The White Food Diet: It cures everything, but it is especially thorough in curing depression, lethargy, insomnia, neuralgia, indigestion, toothache, lack of discipline, failure of will, confusion, bewilderment, awe, bemusement, and obesity.

Five Applications of the Ogives and Gymnopédies: Cures nose polyps. Prolonged applications cure liver disorders and rheumatic pain.

Throwing an Acrobat Out the Window and Founding a New Reli-

gious Sect of Which You Are the High Priest: This cures heart sickness and broken hearts.

A NOTE ON THE PASSIONS

The passions are currently divided up into three categories: the passion for wealth, the passion for glory, and the passion for debauchery. Artists possess the passion for glory. The passions are generally imprudent and unhealthy. Passion leads to excessive ambition, and those who suffer from excessive ambition become pale, gaunt, bald, breathless insomniacs with heart murmurs, melancholy monomania, and stomach inflammation, and eventually die of cancer or apoplexy.

Those susceptible to ambition are bilious or bilious-sanguine and melancholic types, who seek jobs above their talents and exceed the boundaries of emulation.

However, since glory is a noble ambition, sometimes concessions must be made to those who thirst for it.

Recommended reading: *The Passions and Their Dangers and Inconveniences for Individuals, the Family and Society*, Dr. Bergeret, 1878; *The Medicine of the Passions*, Dr. Descuret, 1842.

HOW TO COPE WITH RISING RENTS

Rents have tripled since the turn of the century. The solution to this problem is simple. Acquire a title. Hyphenate your name. Buy a pair of cuff links and have engraved on them the motto: "To live is to act." When you enter and leave your apartment building, be seen carrying Paul Leroy-Beaulieu's bestseller, *The Art of Investing and Managing One's Fortune*, and Louis Reybaud's potboiler, *Jerome Paturot in Search of a Social Position*. Sit in prominent cafés and read these books.

ADVICE ABOUT INTERIOR DECORATING

Each room should be decorated in a different style. For example: the dining room, Renaissance; the drawing room, Eighteenth Century; and the library, Empire. Painters simply use different colors in each room. Whistler had a blue dining room with darker blue dado and doors, a yellow-and-white drawing room, and a gray-and-black studio. My way is to have only one room. Only a bed fits, so I use it as a table.

The other problem with having rooms is that you must have furniture. Caned chairs are popular, but I prefer the washable beech kind one finds in hotels. Chests and four-poster beds are quaint extravagances. I recommend that plywood be used instead of furniture. If you must have your Victorian armchair, your pompadour, your English or Polish armchair, your Louis XIII, your bentwood, or your old oak François I, do not buy the real thing. Buy a cheap imitation at the Bon Marché or Galeries Nanciennes. For example, a real Renaissance sideboard costs 600 francs. At the Bon Marché, an imitation costs 300 francs. I personally recommend the Henri II sideboard, which only costs 180 francs.

If you want bric-a-brac—enameled miniatures and porcelain—don't buy it at antique shops. They make it new, throw a little dirt on it, call it old, and sell it at ten times the cost.

Wallpaper is a delicate business. I am enamored of the enormous mural scenes like *The Lyons-Saint Etienne Railway* or *Hunting in the Forest.* But these are becoming increasingly difficult to find. Avoid those wallpapers that try to look like silk.

THE BEAU BRUMMEL THEORY OF FASHION

Velvet is out. The only truly tasteful suit to wear is black, and is without decoration. The true man is distinguished by the cut of the cloth. Differences are subtle. The cut should follow the natural line of the body. If you want to express yourself further, employ the neckcloth.

The embroidered jacket the Breton peasants popularized is embarrassingly joyful. Do not be caught wearing it. The habit of wearing three or four waistcoats is also frowned upon.

A passerby might think you're a smuggler. Turkish boots are silly. Cossack waistcoats and short English coats are ludicrous. Gold buttons catch the light.

Women squander their money and looks wearing kimono coats and dyeing their hair the color of cows' tails and egg yolks. They pile leaves, flowers, fruit, ribbons, and feathers on their heads and call them hats. Women, don't do it. Wear culottes and Coco Chanel's soft, loose clothes made from jersey. Cut your hair short and wear trousers.

TUBERCULAR WOMEN

The fashion for women is to be skinny and frail and white and sickly-looking. Women are only attractive now if they are dying of tuberculosis. We've had a war. A certain amount of romanticism has been revived.

MYOPIA IN PAINTERS

Only fifteen percent of the general population is short-sighted. But fifty percent of painters are short-sighted. This explains modern art.

LE JOURNAL

My favorite newspaper is *Le Journal.* Their stories are full of pornography, perversion, adultery, sadism, xenophobia, nationalism, anti-Semitism, and scandals. They are a literary journal. Their main concern is that women flirt too much.

PASTEUR'S FAVORITE BOOKS

Pasteur's favorite books were Joseph Droz's *The Art of Being Happy* and Smiles's *Self-Help.* He read these when he was recovering from a cerebral hemorrhage. He suffered the hemorrhage from overwork. Pasteur proved that illness was not caused by weakness of character but by microbes.

THE COURTSHIP OF
VICTOR HUGO'S NIECE

When Camille Flammarion was fifteen, he fell in love with Victor Hugo's niece. He courted her until she left her husband. They spent their honeymoon in a balloon. When he was old enough, he took a young girl as a lover, and the three of them lived together.

RENANISM

Renan wrote *The Life of Jesus* in a Lebanese hut. Clemenceau says he made us what we are. Renanism is a mixture of seriousness, mockery, unctuousness, and blasphemy, resulting in a dilettantism that is taken to the point of nihilism. Renan has been accused of transforming God into an interior decorator.

HAVING A CAR OR HAVING
A CHILD

Much is said these days about whether to own a car or a child. Here are some things to consider:

Owning a car increases your likelihood of divorce, and increases the tendency toward installment-buying. Once you own a car, you will want another. If you own a child, you may not want another. Cars make loud growling and grating noises. Children make loud keening and gurgling noises. A car is less likely to criticize or judge you when it gets older. A car does not require a dowry or an education. A car will expand your movement. A child will limit it.

THE VIRTUES OF SPORT

I approve of sport because it has given women the legal right to wear trousers. Sport is not a way of stimulating national prowess, improving health, taming violence, or disciplining youth. Sport is not always athletic. It may be spectator. Regional sport reflects each countryside's choice of which animal to do violence against. The North enjoys cockfighting, the South bullfighting, the West hunting.

Sport is not English. Tennis began in France. So did hockey. Fencing and boules also began in France.

Gymnastics has become militaristic because it lends itself to movements in unison. The Swedish method emphasizes individual agility.

Cycling is France's most popular sport. Cycle manufacturers were able to make so much money from it that they were willing to promote it. It also provided new opportunities for gambling. Horse racing is also a popular vehicle for gambling.

THE CONFLICT OF REASON AND PASSION

The Greeks invented it. Before them, people did not distinguish between dream and reality, symbol and what it symbolized, body and soul, body and clothes, foot and footprints, shoe and shoeprints.

THE BRETON QUESTION

What is it?

ANGLOPHILISM

If you want to be an Anglophile, at every opportunity refer to your clothes as spencers, jerseys, waterproofs, macintoshes, and mcfarlanes. Tie your tie the way the English do. Carry your cane and mount your horse the way they do. Go to a tavern instead of a café. Be cold to strangers instead of polite. Attend the Jockey Club and gamble on horses. Dress your children in Queen Anne clothes. Be seen reading Miss M. S. Cummings's and Mrs. Elizabeth Wetherell's best-selling novels. Be funny, not witty. Drink beer, not cognac. At every opportunity, use the words *beefsteak, fashionable, lunch, dandy, corned beef, pyjama, high life, baby, cocktail, breakfast, flirt, five o'clock tea, smoking, grill room,* and *shorts.* Send your sons to the Paris School of Political Sciences. Teach them to have pride and tenacity, a practical business sense, and the ability to concentrate on their ambitions and achieve their goals.

HOW TO BECOME A BOURGEOIS

It is not how much money you make that makes you bourgeois, it's how you earn the money and how you spend it.

First, lay the tablecloth symmetrically. Serve dinner in its own room, not in the kitchen. Create a salon. Furnish it with a piano, paintings, candelabras, clocks and bibelots. Receive visitors there.

Pay for your children to go to secondary school, and make sure they take up bourgeois professions. Your sons should achieve the baccalaureate. Provide your daughters with a dowry. Acquire a cultural education.

Know Latin and speak classical French. Do not allow your wife to work. Your quarrel with the church is about politics, not ethics. You believe that morality in women means chastity, fidelity, and duty.

Choose a profession that allows you to wear a dark suit. In other words, no manual labor or physically dirty work. In your manner, be polite. Give a good impression. Cultivate distinction. Be conservative and understated. Don't try to outdo other bourgeois. Simply keep up with them.

HOW TO CHOOSE YOUR COGNAC FROM A VARIEGATED FLASK

When you ask for a cognac in a neighborhood café, the waiter will try to serve you the top portion. You want the bottom portion because it contains more cognac. So insist on being served the bottom portion. Be discreet. If the waiter objects, pour out the top portion, serve yourself the bottom portion, and pour the remaining liquid back into the flask.

LOVE AT FIRST SIGHT

If your parents fell in love the moment they met and insisted on marrying against all odds, you will be condemned to a life of heartbreak, cuckoldry, bachelorhood, and emotional violence that you should avoid at all costs. Do not marry. Do not take a lover.

THE DIFFICULTIES OF LEARNING RUSSIAN

If you are a shipbroker from Honfleur, it is essential that you learn languages. German, Portuguese, Spanish, Italian, Dutch, Danish, Latin, and Greek are easy to learn, but Russian is impossible. Try as you may, you will not learn Russian. You can work as a translator, in Paris at the Foreign Ministry or at an insurance company, you can publish poems and articles on music in which you take Rossini's side against Wagner, but you will not learn Russian.

SPANISH PAINTERS

I befriend Spanish painters because we both must endure the same paradox in our lives—we like spicy food but we lack color in our palette.

THE COLOR WHITE

Isis' color is white. Sugar, grated bones, salt, mildew, cotton, and fish without skin are white. Peladan was killed yesterday by a tainted oyster. The oyster was white. In my music, I always long for white.

FAUCET SALESMEN'S MUSIC

Faucet salesmen's music should endeavour always to keep the tap running. The water which comes out of this tap should be clear and sweet and simple. The faucet itself should be free of rust and should make no sounds. Only the water should make sounds. Then the faucets will be easily sold. Only the faucet salesman knows the secret of his own music.

THE DUTIES AND RESPONSIBILITIES OF A CONTRAPUNTIST

To create music in which tedium is concealed behind malevolent harmonies. To greet poverty, who arrives like a sad little girl with large green eyes. To abandon charming and deeply inept music for boring and uninterestingly competent music. To sit by graciously while you are discovered through music you wrote twenty years ago, while the music you write as a contrapuntist goes unlistened to. To make poverty an aesthetic principle. To search for beauty through a minimum of means. To be tried, fined, and sentenced on libel charges for defending your music. To become a progenitor of sublimities. To resign from the high priesthood of the Cult of the Wound in the Left Shoulder of Our Lord Jesus Christ. To suffer being called a lunatic and being rejected three times from the Academy. To guard against the inflation of the spirit. To eat only white food. To end all ongoing quarrels with your brother and Willy. To face destitution honorably and move to the suburbs. To watch out for scorpions. To die of boredom and fail at everything you do. To squeeze the tips of your own fingers to make yourself cry. To resign from your post in the Arceuil Soviet. To acquire and quarrel with protégés. To discover warlike love. To utilize telepathy whenever possible. To walk around your work several times until you can get it to go with you. To arrive yourself. To devise an elaborate system of shellfish. To exercise ironical conformism. To advertise the virtues of the phonometer. To lecture on musicality among animals. To reveal the lack of truth in art. To take your fingers out of your mouth. To succeed beyond your wildest dreams.

BOOK ONE:

TRIBES AND TRIBESMEN

THE ANCIENT POST-IMPRESSIONISTS OF PARIS

The Post-Impressionists were a nomadic tribe of painters who only lived in direct sunlight. Like their grandfathers before them, the Impressionists, they insisted on scientific accuracy. They allowed no spontaneity, inspiration, or temperament in their work. They wanted to paint what they saw. A tribe member named Degas saw women bathing in tubs in small rooms. He painted them without spontaneity. A tribesman named Monet saw a cathedral and painted it at different times during the day when the light looked different. Clemenceau, a leader of all the Paris tribes, showed him a lily pond, and on his command, Monet painted that to be shown in a room called the Orangerie. They didn't paint the way the woman in the tub looked to them, or the way the cathedral or the lily pond made them feel; they painted the way the light looked on these objects. I say objects because that's all they were to these Post-Impressionist tribesmen. Painted without spontaneity, inspiration, or temperament, a woman or a lily pond is just an object that attracts light.

The Post-Impressionist tribesmen didn't realize the apocalyptic character of their painting. So when people complained that the women in Degas's paintings weren't women, they were just objects, Degas didn't say, yes, that's my point exactly. He said that these women were simple folk concerned with their physical condition. And when the Americans and English said that they were not nude, they were naked, the French didn't know what to say because they don't make that distinction. They have one word for both conditions.

But the Post-Impressionist tribesmen did not agree about everything. They agreed that they should paint the way the light looked on objects, they agreed that women were objects, and they agreed that there should be no spontaneity, temperament, or inspiration in their canvases. But they did not agree on where to put their canvases in a particular room. When two of the elder tribesmen, Rodin and Monet, tried to put their work together in the room called the Georges-Petit Gallery, Rodin insisted on keeping all the best locations in the room for himself, and his tribesman Monet got very angry. Rodin blamed the argument on Monet, and the two tribesmen did not speak to each other for a long time, despite their common interest in medieval architecture.

THE ORIGIN OF CÉZANNE'S POWER

Cézanne did not depend so much on the light; he liked to paint things over and over again the way Monet painted the cathedral.

Cézanne lived in the foothills near the Mediterranean, far away from Paris. He preferred to paint Mont Saint-Victoire over and over again. Nobody knew why. The Symbolist and Nabi tribes liked his paintings, but they didn't understand them. Cézanne didn't try to explain. What he did say didn't make much sense.

Cézanne didn't paint the way the light hit the objects. He painted the forms he saw in the objects. He didn't do anything but work. He couldn't use models because he was embarrassed to hire them. As a result, his nudes are oddly shaped.

Eventually, when they put all his paintings in a room in Paris called the Ambroise Vollard Gallery, painters from the other tribes thought they understood what he was doing. They didn't. At least they recognized the importance of his work.

I appreciated Cézanne's paintings and created my own tribe called Cubists. The Fauve tribe also credits Cézanne with their innovations.

THE SYMBOLISTS' REVOLT

Some members of the Post-Impressionist tribe decided that there should be inspiration, spontaneity, and temperament in art after all. They decided to break with the Post-Impressionist tribe and start a new one called the Symbolists. They believed that painting should be a synthesis of feeling and form. The Post-Impressionists said the Romantics had already done that, but the Symbolists thought painting should express this idea, not explain it, as the Romantic tribe of their great-great-grandfathers had done.

Only two of the tribesmen actually showed these ideas in their paintings. These tribesmen were called Gauguin and Redon. The other tribesmen developed elaborate rituals to express these ideas. The rituals were called manifestoes. The tribesmen would write down their ideas in elaborate word paintings. Then a group of tribesmen would convene in a place called a salon and chant these word paintings at each other, or make up new word paintings about the ones they had just chanted. These word paintings would also be printed in collections called newspapers and books and sent to men of other tribes. The men would read them and shout word paintings for or against the Symbolist word paintings. This ritual was not new; many previous tribes had performed it.

Some of the word paintings from other tribes contained interesting ideas. Henri Bergson, a tribesman from an international tribe called Philosophers, said that intuition was the only path to knowledge and art the only way to depict that path. Charcot and Freud, who belonged to an international tribe called Psychologists, argued the importance of dreams and psychic life. The Symbolist tribesmen repeated these word paintings to prove they were right. Gustave Kahn, of the international tribe called Critics, said introspection knows no limits. Mallarmé, a tribesman who made word paintings called Poetry, said art should reveal the mysterious meanings and aspects of existence.

THE ORACLE'S ANSWER

That tribe called Critics, who made word paintings about the tribes and tribesmen who made art, claimed four painters as the true grandfathers of the Symbolist tribe: Gustave Moreau, Puvis de Chavannes, Odilon Redon, and Eugène Carrière. Moreau lived on the slopes of Montmartre, never came down, and never put his paintings together in a room where people could see them. Puvis de Chavannes painted murals which were too large to be put in a room. Redon was well-known and well-loved by the Symbolist tribesmen. He put his paintings in a room with them called the Durand-Ruel.

PAUL GAUGUIN DEFINES HAPPINESS

Gauguin was still a member of the Post-Impressionist tribe when he left for Panama and Martinique. When he returned, he was a Symbolist. He had found pure color and expressive power. A trip to a hot country can change a painter this way. In a big room in Paris called the Exposition of 1889, he saw prehistoric art from Central and South America. These are hot places. No one in Paris had seen this art in a room before. Gauguin liked it very much. He said he had savage blood. His family had settled in the hot country of Peru, and he had grown up in Lima. He wanted to paint with power from the hot countries. People said painters with that power belonged to an international tribe called Primitives.

Gauguin painted experiences not explainable by the senses. The Naturalist and Impressionist tribesmen would not have done that. This is what made him a Symbolist tribesman when he came back from the hot countries.

Gauguin could not stay in Paris. He went to other wild places, some hot and wet like Polynesia, some cold and wet like Brittany, some temperate like Arles, but all wild and emotional. Gauguin craved wildness and emotions. Of the emotions, Gauguin liked unsatisfied desire best. He liked to depict the fox because it was the Indian symbol for perversity.

After six years in the Symbolist tribe, Gauguin had spent all his money painting. At the Exposition of 1889, he put all his work in a room called the Café des Arts with other paintings by Symbolist tribesmen. This was the first time the Symbolist tribesmen had put their paintings together in a room. Gauguin didn't make any money. He moved to Tahiti, where he painted both satisfied and unsatisfied desire. He had an auction and sold a painting to Degas. Aurier wrote a word painting about the auction and published it in a newspaper called the *Mercure de France.* Now people knew who Gauguin was. That was a good thing, since tribesmen don't like it when another tribesman leaves Paris. They tend to ignore him or misunderstand him or forget about him or dislike him as they had with Cézanne. But people liked Gauguin's Tahitian paintings better than his French paintings, the same way they preferred Rousseau's jungle paintings to his French paintings, even though they're the same paintings. They want to see the exotic, but they want it painted in Paris.

No one liked Gauguin's Tahitian paintings when they were first put together in a room in Paris in 1893. He hadn't painted these pictures in Paris. He didn't live in Paris, and he used new colors. Strindberg, who belonged to the tribe of Playwrights, called him an inferior to Puvis de Chavannes. Gauguin said that Puvis explained his idea but didn't paint it. To Gauguin, each color had its own scent. Each scent had its corresponding color. Color vibrated the way musical notes do.

In 1903, Gauguin died in the Marquesas Islands. In 1906, his work was put together in a room in Paris called the Salon d'Automne. The new Fauve tribe saw it and especially liked it. The new Expressionist tribe in Germany also liked Gauguin. Mirbeau says his work reveals the irony of sorrow, which is the threshold of mystery.

THE STORY OF VAN GOGH

Van Gogh's paintings were so expressive that a new tribe formed and called themselves the Expressionists. Van

Gogh wanted to paint what he felt. He was unteachable and self-taught. His family came from international tribes of Pastors and Art Dealers. Van Gogh had trouble growing up among them; he got along with neither. Before he joined the Symbolist tribe, Van Gogh tried to work for the Art Dealers called Goupil & Co. He failed. He tried to work as a missionary with Belgian miners. He failed again. When he painted, he thought he was failing too, but he kept painting. He didn't stop. He couldn't believe anything other people told him, so he had to discover everything for himself. He moved to Paris to live with his brother Theo, who belonged to the Art Dealer tribe. He began to find his own colors. He began to find his own paintings. He began to express himself the way he wanted. He saw Impressionist and Divisionist paintings and Japanese prints, and took what he needed from these. He met Gauguin. He painted flat areas of unbroken, pure color. They expressed him the way he wanted.

Van Gogh was cranky and fought with everyone in Paris. In 1888, he moved to Arles, a hilly place away from Paris and closer to Aix and the Mediterranean. He was alone. He drank a lot. He worked a lot. It was calm.

GAUGUIN AND VAN GOGH COME INTO CONFLICT

Gauguin arrived in Arles in December. Van Gogh quarreled with him about aesthetics and values. Van Gogh attacked Gauguin, then cut his own ear. Van Gogh had frightened himself. He admitted himself to an asylum. He did not feel better. He shot himself.

In 1901, they put all Van Gogh's paintings in a room in Paris called the Bernheim-Jeune Gallery. This is why the Fauves started their tribe. They put his paintings in rooms in Amsterdam in 1905, in Cologne in 1912, and in Berlin in 1914. This is why the Expressionists started their tribes.

In 1913, Van Gogh's nephew published Van Gogh's word paintings to his brother. Painters in the Paris tribes read them.

THE CONQUEST OF THE NABIS

After Gauguin left for Tahiti, Bernard and Denis started their own tribe called the Nabis. They admired Gauguin's work and its sources in medieval sculpture, Japanese prints, and primitive art. Many painters from other tribes lack respect for the Nabis. They say that they are only a French version of the decorative Art Nouveau tribe, and simply a path from Symbolism to Expressionism. The path from Symbolism to Expressionism is not simple.

Bernard was the first to arrange Van Gogh's paintings in a room. It was called the Gallery of Le Barc de Boutteville. He did this not long after Van Gogh died. The Nabis put their paintings together in a room called the Café Volponi in 1889.

The Nabi tribe had their own ritual. They met in secret at a monthly dinner, where they wore costumes and enacted ceremonies similar to those of the international Rosicrucian religious tribe. They talked about paintings, theosophy, and eastern religions. They named themselves Nabis. They put their paintings together in the room called the Gallery of Le Barc de Boutteville every year during the 1890's. Until someone put Cézanne's paintings together in a room in Paris in the 1890's and the Fauve tribe put theirs together in the room called the Salon d'Automne in 1905, the Nabis's work was the most original and alarming anyone had seen in Paris.

PARIS DISMISSES BONNARD AND VUILLARD

Some people say Vuillard and Bonnard belonged to the Nabi tribe. They didn't. Not every painter belonged to a tribe. Tribesmen wanted them to belong. Tribesmen wanted to understand the painters who worked alone. Sometimes they didn't understand.

Vuillard's and Bonnard's work looked like the paintings of the Symbolist tribesmen, the Nabis, and even the Fauves. They painted secrets in the form of small corners of rooms or parks with a person or two together inside. But regardless of the objects they chose, they painted the secret mystery of those objects. Bonnard became very good at it.

THE BONES OF TOULOUSE-LAUTREC

Toulouse-Lautrec did not belong to a tribe. He would have been a sportsman, but he broke his legs and they never grew up like he did. He grew up a dwarf and frequented Montmartre dance halls. He drew, painted, and studied them. When you looked at his paintings, you felt at least eight different unpleasant, conflicting sensations. Toulouse-Lautrec did not allow censure or caricature in his work. He captured the disillusionment and excitement of the cabaret.

Toulouse-Lautrec used an aspect of Japanese prints in his paintings that no one else had used. The Impressionist tribesmen had used their manner. Degas and Monet had used their space. Gauguin and Van Gogh had used their colors and patterns. Toulouse-Lautrec used their way of conveying movement within flat, linear patterns.

Painters respected Toulouse-Lautrec when he was alive. He showed his paintings, posters, and lithographs for ten years in a room called the Indépendants. He died in 1901. He was thirty-seven.

Toulouse-Lautrec painted with oil on cardboard. He didn't steam his pencils into syrup the way Degas did. When I first came to Paris, I discovered Toulouse-Lautrec. It made a difference to me.

MAILLOL REDUCED TO SUBJECTION

Maillol does not belong to a tribe. People say he belonged to the Nabis. He came to Paris from a fishing village called Banyuls near the Spanish border. Vuillard convinced Vollard to cast Maillol's wood and terra-cotta statuettes in bronze and put them together in a room in Paris in 1902. Gauguin and Rodin admired them. In 1905, they put them together in Paris in a bigger room called the Salon d'Automne, where many people admired them. Gide said Maillol's sculpture *Mediterranean* was beautiful because it signified nothing.

SIEGE OF THE FAUVES

There are several Expressionist tribes. The Fauves are one. *Fauve* means wild beast. When Vauxcelles, from the Critics tribe, said "wild beasts," he meant the colors, not the painters. Everyone misunderstood.

Matisse, Derain, and Vlaminck were Fauves. In 1905, they put their paintings together in a room in Paris called the Salon d'Automne. Matisse was thirty-six.

The Fauves tried to make their colors bolder, surfaces flatter, brushwork more chaotic, and feelings more expressive than any Symbolists or Nabis had. They admired Cézanne, Van Gogh, and Gauguin, and wanted to continue their discoveries. They introduced deliberate color disharmonies. They refused to draw contours. Both color and composition were planned. They insisted on the integrity of feeling. They depended on intuition and instinct. They admired Islamic and African art, and how these reflected cultures outside Europe. No one else admired cultures outside Europe. People were shocked when they saw these cultures admired in Fauve paintings. Elie Faure, a tribesman from the Critics, tried to make people aware. He said, "Look at these paintings anyway."

THE RADICAL DEVOTION OF MATISSE

In a word painting about his own art, Matisse said that his feelings and his way of expressing them were inextricable. Matisse left the Fauve tribe to paint other pictures. In these pictures he found a balance between what he felt and how he painted. He made colors move. He condensed meaning. He followed the desire of the line. No one joined his new tribe.

THE REBELLION OF KANDINSKY

Kandinsky was a Russian painter who lived in Munich and belonged to his own tribe. In 1910 he asked me and Braque and some Fauves to put our paintings together in a room with his in Munich. It was the biggest collection of work from the new international tribes that anyone had put together in one room. In 1912, he published a word painting book called *Concerning the Spiritual in Art*, which explains why paintings do not need to represent objects. Kandinsky was upset after Rutherford bombarded the atom and discovered that substances don't really exist. It was important to Kandinsky to show emotions and spiritual essences in his paintings.

In 1912, Kandinsky put paintings by himself, Klee, and Marc together in rooms all over Europe. These paintings did not represent objects. He called this his Blue Rider Exhibit. Everyone noticed. Kandinsky published a series of word painting books called *The Blue Rider Almanac*. In one he reprinted Rousseau paintings.

In 1913, Kandinsky put his painting called *Improvisation No. 30* in a room in London. Roger Fry, from the international tribe of Critics, called it pure visual music and said that it expresses emotion without representing anything.

THE CULT OF ROUSSEAU

Rousseau wanted to paint poorly but couldn't. He painted well in spite of himself. People call this Primitivism. For most of the painters from the other tribes, the problem is reversed. We try to paint well. If we don't try, we paint very poorly. We don't want to paint poorly.

Kandinsky said that Rousseau's reality was greater than ours. Rousseau put his paintings together from 1886 to 1910 in a room in Paris called the Salon des Indépendants.

Rousseau dislocated each piece of an object from its adjacent pieces and showed them side by side. He was the first painter to do this. I was the second. He made the objects that were important to him bigger than the objects that weren't. Pierre Loti's forehead was very important. So was his hand. His cigarette was not. Neither was his cat. Rousseau's objects lock together in a geometric design which the viewer cannot detach.

Rousseau admired Japanese prints. Rain slashes diagonally across his first jungle painting. Rousseau conveyed his feelings in his paintings. Rousseau felt whimsy and magic.

CUBISM DEFENDS ITSELF

Form creates space. I started the Cubist tribe. In 1907, Braque saw my painting *Les Demoiselles d'Avignon*. In 1908, we put our paintings together in a room called the Salon d'Automne. Apollinaire said our work was composed of tiny cubes. Then he said that Matisse had said it. Later, Gleizes and Metzinger said that form is inseparable from the space it creates. We admired Cézanne. In 1910 and 1911, Braque and I painted the same pictures. We painted the forms as we thought them, not as we saw them. We didn't use colors. Braque put sand, sawdust, and metal filings into his paint. Then the paint had form. I pasted a piece of oilcloth to my canvas.

In March 1911, Gleizes, Metzinger, and some other Cubist tribesmen put their paintings together in Room No. 41 of the Salon des Indépendants. The other tribes noticed the work. In 1912, Gleizes and Metzinger published a word painting called *On Cubism*. In October 1912, a group from the Cubist tribe put their paintings together in a room at the Galerie de la Boëtie. They called it the Salon de la Section d'Or. Some of the older Cubists wouldn't let Marcel Duchamp exhibit his *Nude Descending a Staircase*. Apollinaire wrote a word painting in 1913 called *Aesthetic Meditations on the Cubist Painters*.

The war started. I left the Cubist tribe.

THE FLIGHT OF MARCEL DUCHAMP

In 1902, when he was only fifteen, Marcel Duchamp joined the Impressionist tribe. In 1907, he joined the Fauve tribe. In 1910, he joined the Cubist tribe. In 1912, when the Cubist tribe refused to let him put his painting *Nude Descending a Staircase* in a room with their paintings, he took his painting home in a taxi. He quit the tribe. He says he will never join another tribe.

In July 1912, Duchamp went to Munich and painted *The King and Queen Surrounded by Swift Nudes*. He came back to Paris in September. In 1913, he started making sculpture from kitchen stools and bicycle wheels. In 1915, he called these ready-mades. He constructed two more called *Pharmacy* and *Bottle Rack*. He began work on a large glass painting called *Bride Stripped Bare by Her Bachelors, Even*. He is developing a new physics, mathematics, and a fourth dimension for the painting. He says that the act of love is an ideal fourth-dimensional situation. In 1913, he made the painting *Coffee Grinder*, which is a study for his *Bride*. He is using glass because he used a glass palette when he painted on canvas and wants to protect the paint from oxidization. He used paraffin to outline the shapes on the glass. He etched them in fluoridic acid. The fumes were too strong, so he stopped. He glued wires with varnish and sealed them with foil. He has made two preliminary studies this way. One is called *Glider*, the other is called *Cemetery of Uniforms and Liveries*. Duchamp created his system of measurements through accidents. He used these to make the *Bride*. The theories of physics he created for the painting are called "oscillating density," "uncontrollable weight," and "emancipated metal."

Duchamp keeps all his notes for the painting in a green cardboard box. He has a large schematic drawing on the wall of his studio where he works out his ideas. Duchamp has a weak heart and couldn't fight in the war. In 1915, he moved to New York. Everyone there already knew him because in 1913 they had put his *Nude Descending a Staircase* in the room called the Armory Show. Everyone was outraged. They didn't think a nude should descend a staircase. Most people think nudes should stand still. They should lounge, or bathe, or reflect. But, above all, they should not descend a staircase.

Marcel Duchamp is the most innovative painter of our time. He will become esteemed. This may take fifty years.

DE CHIRICO AND THE DOLPHIN

De Chirico was in Paris from 1911 to 1915. He started a tribe with Carra called the Metaphysical School. He painted canvases of people dreaming in deserted squares, read Nietzsche, and wrote a word painting against Impressionism.

De Chirico was Italian, grew up in Greece, and lived in Munich. He believed Nietzsche when he said that underneath the reality in which we live, another altogether different reality lies concealed.

De Chirico said his art consists of two lonelinesses, the plastic loneliness and the metaphysical loneliness.

BOOK TWO:
CUSTOMS OF THE PARIS TRIBES

SACRIFICIAL BULLS

Stein bought most of her paintings from Vollard, on the Boulevard Lafitte. They had a buying-and-selling ritual that they performed together. Vollard did not show the pictures he had for sale. He turned them against the wall and piled them in stacks. Stein would come in and ask to see a Cézanne landscape. Vollard would go upstairs and return with a Cézanne nude. Stein would ask again to see a Cézanne landscape. Vollard would go upstairs and come down with a Cézanne still life. Stein would ask again to see a Cézanne landscape. Vollard would bring down a half-painted landscape. Stein would ask to see a completely painted landscape. Vollard would bring down a green landscape. Stein would ask to see a yellow Cézanne landscape. They went on like this until Vollard made Stein laugh. Then she would buy two pictures.

If Stein got impatient, she would go to Fouquet's, eat honey cakes and nut candies, and come back. If she was really unhappy, she would go to Fouquet's, buy a bowl of strawberry jam, and not come back.

THE COST OF ENTERTAINING

When Gertrude Stein had lunch at the Matisses', they ate jugged hare in the manner of Perpignan and a Madeira wine called Roncio. Matisse brought Derain to one of these lunches. He and Gertrude Stein did not like each other.

Rousseau had lunch with Vollard and a professor. When he finished eating, he took out his sketchbook and began to draw. He liked the light and the white walls in the cellar, and the way the figures looked against them.

When Matisse had dinner at Gertrude Stein's, Hélène-the-Cook would fry the eggs instead of making an omelet.

ARABIAN SPICES

Mallarmé had people over on Tuesday nights, beginning in 1884. These became known simply as "Tuesdays." The Goncourts started having people over the next year, and this became known as the Goncourts' "attic."

Gauguin had his soirées on Saturday nights in the 1890's, when he was back from Tahiti. Degas, Strindberg, and Mallarmé came. Rousseau came uninvited. He lived down the block. He played his violin. He offered to help Degas to get exhibited. Degas complained about the difficulties.

Gertrude Stein had her gatherings on Saturday nights. Germans, Hungarians, Americans, and Spaniards came. Everyone brought someone. People danced and looked at the canvases. Once, I got in a fight with Fernande about the difference between painters and Apaches. Rousseau was afraid to knock at the door. A Scandinavian came and, instead of coming up, would stand in the courtyard.

TACTICS

At the Salon des Refusés in 1863, Manet showed his *Déjeuner sur l'Herbe.* Napoleon III didn't like it.

At the Salon des Champs-Elysées in 1885, Rousseau showed two paintings, *An Italian Dance* and *Thunder.* Spectators slashed them with knives. Afterward, the paintings were taken out of the show and exhibited with the Refusés.

The exhibition of the Société des Artistes Indépendants in 1886 was their second show. Their first show failed because the tribesmen stole their own money to buy fishing rods. But at the 1886 exhibit, Seurat showed his *Summer Sunday at Grande Jatte,* and Rousseau showed his *Night of the Carnival* and *Thunder* again. Works by Signac and Redon were also exhibited. Seurat was accused of imitating Chavannes.

At the Salon d'Automne of 1905, Cézanne, Derain, Braque, Roualt, Vlaminck, Friesz, Vuillard, and Dufy all showed work. Rousseau showed his *Hungry Lion.* Matisse showed his *Woman with the Hat.* Vauxcelles named the Fauves. Maillol showed his *Mediterranean* and it was very popular. People laughed at Matisse's *Woman with the Hat* and tried to scratch it. Gertrude Stein bought it. She didn't understand why they were laughing at it. Matisse went the first day and heard what people said about his *Woman with the Hat.* He never went back. He sent his wife instead.

At the Salon de la Nationale in 1912, José Maria Sert exhibited a large dining room ceiling.

At the Futurist exhibit in 1913, Boccioni showed a construction containing human hair, glass eyes, and fragments of a staircase.

MUMMIES

The Sun Went Down Over the Adriatic: This canvas was painted entirely by movements of Lolo the donkey's tail. It was exhibited at the Salon des Indépendants.

THE FESTIVAL OF THE PHOENIX

Rite of Spring, May 29, 1913, at the Théâtre des Champs-Elysées: The Théâtre des Champs-Elysées had just opened. Denis and Vuillard had painted it. The theater was full. The audience wore pearls, aigrettes, ostrich plumes, tail coats, and tulle. According to Cocteau, there was snobbism, countersnobbism, and supersnobbism. The audience shouted, whistled, booed, and hooted so loudly that the dancers couldn't hear the music. Countesses thought they were being made fun of.

Parade, May 18, 1917, Paris: The curtain I painted went up to the "Prelude of the Red Curtain," composed by Satie and dedicated to me. The curtain was painted with a scene of circus performers lounging around. Then the First Manager tried to get everyone's attention by dancing a repetitive dance to repetitive music. His costume was ten feet high and made more noise than the music. I made the costumes. Then the Chinese Prestidigitator came in. He was dressed in vermilion, yellow, and black. Massine played him. He bowed, ate fire, and had an egg which vanished and reappeared. Then a mime came in. He brought the American Manager with him. He was wearing a skyscraper costume on his back. He stamped around the stage. The Little American Girl came on stage and danced the Steamship Rag. She pretended to catch a train, drive a car, swim, act in a movie, and botch a holdup. Sound effects accompanied each mimed act. The Third Manager came in on a horse. He had no music. He introduced the two Acrobats. They tumbled while a waltz with xylophones played. The Managers tried to prevent the crowd of people from leaving. The people left anyway. The Managers fell down. The Girl cried. The Chinese Prestidigitator didn't do anything.

THE COMPOSITION OF PARIS

I lived in the rue Ravignan. To get to my studio you had to pass a steep stairway that led down to the studio Max

Jacob was about to occupy, and a second steep passageway that would take you to another studio. My friend had killed himself there. Beyond these was the big door to my studio. It smelled like paint and animals. I had a couch, a stove, and some chairs, but no one ever sat down.

I lived on the Boulevard Clichy. We had furniture and a servant who served soufflés. The apartment was sunny, and Braque came over for tea. I had an apartment in rue Schoelcher which overlooked a cemetery. I had an apartment on Boulevard Raspail above Victor Hugo's tree. When I lived in a little house in Montrouge, I had on my bed a red silk counterpane that had been given to me by a Chilean society woman.

Gertrude Stein lived at 27 rue de Fleurus. The place consisted of a four-room pavilion on two stories and a studio. Before the war the studio was separate from the pavilion. After the war it was connected by a passageway. The entryway led to a dining room filled with books. Where there weren't books, there were drawings and paintings hung. The studio was locked with a Yale key. No one else in the neighborhood had them. French keys were much bigger. The studio had large Renaissance furniture. The big table sat in the middle of the room. It had an inkstand and French student notebooks and Alice's earthquake pictures all over it. There was a cast iron stove in the studio. There was another table in the corner of the room where we emptied our pockets of whatever nails, pebbles, pipes and cigarette holders we had collected on our walks. The chairs had legs so high you couldn't get your feet to rest on the floor. Gertrude let hers hang. Alice sat on hers. The studio had high, whitewashed walls and gas lamps. Gertrude hung most of our paintings in there.

THE SEVEN CONSPIRATORS

Gertrude Stein liked to collect breakable objects. She divided women into three types: Indoor Women, Decorative Women, and Women of Intrigue. I used to worry that I might look like the American president Lincoln. Alice tried to fix her hair like his. Fernande spoke Montmartois and talked about hats, furs, dogs, and perfume. Max Jacob and Apollinaire kissed ladies' hands. Marie Laurencin made frightening animal noises. Van Dongen's wife was a vegetarian and ate only spinach. I was afraid of his daughter, who crushed me when she hugged me. Vollard had a lisp. He stood in the doorway of his gallery with his arms stretched across the doorjamb so no one could come in. Gertrude Stein wrote late at night and slept until noon. It irritated her a great deal when people beat their rugs in the courtyard. Gertrude Stein loved the hot sun and would sit out under it even in Spain. Erik Satie could not get along with his fellow musicians, so he only had friends who were painters. After his seclusion, he befriended Braque, Derain, Léger, Brancusi, and myself. He wrote everything down in his notebook, even the directions on street signs.

THE ORACLE SPEAKS

Gertrude Stein said that Cubism was Spanish. She said only the Americans and the Spanish understood Abstraction, the Americans through disembodiment and the Spanish through ritual. Rousseau said that the couch was not in the jungle, that the jungle was in Yadwigha's dream. He said he kept his naïveté because M. Gérôme told him to keep it. He said that we were masters, I in the Egyptian style and he in the modern. Matisse said you have to seek the desire of the line. Max Jacob said that personality is a persistent error. Degas said Gustave Moreau wanted us to believe that the gods wore watch chains. Vlaminck said he loved Van Gogh better than his own father. Robert Mortier, a distinguished billiard theorist, said that no man is a prophet in his own country.

Brief Lives by Henri Matisse

INTRODUCTION

I name the biographies set forth here Brief Lives. The reasons are many. Some of the artists portrayed in the following pages are still mere boys, and the lives they have lived so far have been brief. Some have achieved brilliance for a short moment, only to falter forever afterward. Others may enjoy fleeting moments of brilliance surrounded by intervals of mediocrity. Some have already died and some may die young. Still others may succumb to a surfeit of grief or bitterness and live out their lives in darkness. Some may enjoy a brief moment of fame or glory, despite the fact that most of their work is pure genius. And still others may have so much to do, so much to discover, so much to invent, that one lifetime is not enough, and even if they live into old age, their lives will be cut short long before their innovations are complete.

HENRI ROUSSEAU

Those people who ridiculed Rousseau only belittled themselves. People made fun of Rousseau because he was not educated in art and was therefore an outsider. Rousseau was not an innocent, but his soul was innocent.

Rousseau never traveled to the jungle in Mexico or anywhere else. Picasso has stolen Rousseau's ideas and many more artists will steal them after the war. But they will not give Rousseau credit for his innovations the way they give Cézanne credit, because they are embarrassed by Rousseau's childlike nature. Even now that Rousseau is dead, other artists are still embarrassed by his ingenuousness, guilelessness, and naïveté, because they are afraid they might be like him. But they are too self-conscious to be like Rousseau. We would all be lucky if we were more like Rousseau. Our art would improve. We would be happy and flourish.

Rousseau understood color much better than Picasso does. Picasso did not discover Rousseau in 1908. He was first esteemed at the 1905 Autumn Salon where Vauxcelles labeled me a Fauve. At his first exhibition in 1885, Rousseau's paintings were slashed.

Rousseau did not begin to paint until after he retired. He took his portraits seriously. Rousseau invented the portrait-landscape. Rousseau painted Marie Laurencin fat because he thought she didn't like him.

Rousseau always believed in ghosts and spirits. All his wives and children died young.

Other artists must deny Rousseau's whimsy in order to deny his genius, so they go on pretending Rousseau was serious. He wasn't. Lawyers produced Rousseau's *Merry Jesters* in court to prove his imbecility, while mothers of artists commissioned him to paint snake charmers. His cows are much too big, his football players cast no shadows. His moon has a face, and his monkeys toss a milk bottle. In particular, the Cubists have stolen his mandolin.

Rousseau told everyone that all great art was Egyptian and all foreigners were American, but this was just a code he used to simplify his speech.

Rousseau always wanted to paint like an academic painter, but he could only paint like himself.

At the end of his life, Rousseau was not afraid to love a woman who did not love him. Max Weber loved him. I loved him and do still.

When Rousseau painted babies, their heads were always much larger than their bodies. This is true of babies.

Rousseau was a man who dreamed awake. All Rousseau's paintings are these waking dreams. No wonder he believed in spirits. If the Hôtel Biron acquires a ghost, it will be his.

AUGUSTE RODIN

The Rodin predicament reminds me very much of The Emperor's New Clothes. In public everyone says what a great master Rodin was, what an artist. But alone in their rooms they are embarrassed. They remember him as a doddering old man who was entirely too interested in certain amorous attributes of the female form. Still, in public they go on pretending he was a great man. The problem is that Rodin just died, and one either dwells on his ignominious old age or finds him impossible to summarize.

Rodin never had enough studios or residences at one time to satisfy him. Even the Hôtel Biron was not enough.

Rodin made his own myth. He pretended to be victimized and guileless and believed his own story. That is how he became bitter and resentful. It makes no difference that Rodin's sister died, or that he grew up in Paris, or that he was rejected by the Ecole des Beaux-Arts, or was exiled to Belgium during the Prussian War. He would have prevailed no matter what happened or failed to happen to him. For many artists life is a series of lucky or unlucky accidents. Rodin was neither lucky nor unlucky. He was singular in purpose.

Rodin is the bridge between two centuries. The old artists can see only the outrageous and incomprehensible future in his *Balzac* and *Gates.* The young artists can see only the insipid and academic past in his *Kiss* and *Eternal Idol.* It seems he can't win, but he has.

The *Gates of Hell* is the most modern of all Rodin's work. Since Rodin is the Hugo and Balzac of French sculpture, it is appropriate that he should have designed their monuments. Rodin knew about African art before I did, he knew about Japanese art before it became popular, and he discovered the secret of Puvis de Chavannes. When people talk about Rodin's work, they like to talk about nature and motion. I have nothing to say about either.

Rodin didn't create his own scandals, but he knew how to

use them to his advantage. Though Rodin denied politics, the *Balzac* affair was really the Dreyfus affair. Likewise, his separate pavilion at the 1900 Exhibition, Hugo's monument, Camille Claudel's incarceration, his reversal on Nijinsky's *Afternoon of a Faun*, the rejection of the *Calais* monument, Rodin's funeral, the possible establishment of a Rodin museum here at the Hôtel Biron, where Rodin allegedly committed sacrilege by exhibiting erotic watercolors in the sacristy—all these were and are political events.

People think that because Rodin's work shows genius, it should also show worldliness and sophistication. They are shocked when it does not. Many of his works were never finished. This is not the point. Incompleteness is a quality of his work, not a fault.

People make too much of the American Duchess. She was not important. She only humiliated Rodin in the short run. Each person assumes only he knows which woman Rodin really loved. A would-be biographer believes that Rodin went to the grave never having known love for a woman. A lady with a fake aristocratic title selects as Rodin's true love an obscure Italian model from his early years in Nice. A former amanuensis insists on some obvious choice like Camille Claudel. An art critic theorizes that Rodin could never love a woman who loved him, or obeyed him, or responded to his advances. A fellow chevalier in the Legion of Honor thinks that Rodin's true love was always Rose.

Rodin never loved anyone but Helen von Nostitz, daughter of Sophie von Hindenburg. I saw him pass her photograph, which rested atop a glass case of fake Egyptian artifacts in his sitting room here at the Hôtel Biron. If you saw the way he gestured toward this photo, so painfully, as if his whole life had been a failure, you would believe me. You would throw away all your other theories.

To Rodin, everything was sex. Art, women, nature, love—everything. Rodin mistreated women, but he did not disrespect them. They were the only thing that mattered. They knew this, and that is why they were susceptible to him. He appealed to their vanity. He also appealed to their sense of mystery. Rodin was one of the few artists—like Michelangelo—who had mystery inside him and didn't have to go looking for it. Instead, he was driven by it. Rodin was only comfortable with art and women. Rodin was capable of loving anyone at all. So it is no wonder that at the end of his life Rodin became openly obsessed with women's most sexual characteristics. From the beginning of his life he had carried a single idea in a single direction—from male warriors to Dante's hell, to Adam and Eve, to fraternities of religious men, to solitary men bigger than life, and this is where it finally and inevitably led him.

Rodin would have been a better artist if he had stayed with Camille Claudel. But either way, Camille Claudel would have been ruined by Rodin. Rodin never had any idea what his sons could have meant to him. Rodin should have loved Nijinsky. He should have had Camille Claudel released from the asylum.

Rodin was a redhead. The redhead has no business trifling with women. The redhead is unkind to all women. If a woman's first love is a redhead, she will never recover.

It makes all the difference in the world what, in Rodin's statue, Balzac is doing under his robe. To Rodin, anything was possible. That is why he was so shocking and so successful. In the future he will be accused of everything.

CAMILLE CLAUDEL

Camille Claudel gained a lot of weight after she had her two sons, but she did not go crazy and her voice did not change. Her sister Louise is jealous of her even now, and incarcerated her to take her money and property, a country house. People say she could have married Debussy. It's true he wanted to marry her, but she could not have married him.

Camille Claudel's *Çacountala* is much warmer than Rodin's *Eternal Idol* and shows a great understanding of what love is.

The *Eternal Idol* does not understand love, only worship, which is a form of hatred.

Camille Claudel's tiny figures called *The Gossipers* and *The Wave* constitute a new kind of art—the art of telling secrets. No one will take up this art for a long time. If Camille Claudel did not have a famous brother and a famous lover, her art might be respected and she might not be incarcerated. We think that Camille Claudel must have made a mistake to have had such an unfortunate life. But she did not make a mistake. We have made one. Because she is a woman, we don't believe in her talent. We indulged her when she was younger, thinking she would go away. When she didn't, her family locked her up. She is more Nijinsky's sister than Paul's. She is more akin to Nijinsky in having the kind of genius people are intent on destroying. If we have learned anything from Camille Claudel and Nijinsky, it is this: if people are intent on destroying your genius, get away from them. Get away from everyone. Do not love anybody. Who can obey this warning?

The reason George Sand could write and take Chopin as a lover and Gwen John can be a painter is that people let them. Camille Claudel does not understand this. Camille Claudel thinks it is through some fault of her own that she is being thwarted and punished. Her blaming Rodin is merely a pretense; in fact, she blames only herself.

I would rather say that Camille Claudel is a great French sculptress than have to say that Camille Claudel is Paul Claudel's sister, was Rodin's student and lover, and has been locked up by her brother, sister, and mother in an asylum, where she does not belong. Do I have to say those things at all? Who is forcing me to say them?

I wish there were some way to get Camille Claudel away from Rodin and her family. Then she could fulfill her art, the art of telling secrets. When women can no longer stand the way they are treated, they will remember Camille Claudel and use her as an example.

EDUARD STEICHEN

Eduard Steichen is the only artist in Paris who constantly does things for other people. For Alfred Stieglitz's 291 Gallery in America, he arranges for shows of French paintings. For Stieglitz's magazine *Camera Work*, he arranges for monographs to be written by the tenants of the Hôtel Biron, and for articles to be written by painters on why they hate photography. For Rodin, he photographs his *Balzac* so that one day other people might understand it. For me, he explains how my paintings utilize the Purjinke effect. For Cocteau, he arranges an introduction to Rilke, so the younger poet might have an older poet to adore. For the Hôtel Biron, he arbitrates discussions among the tenants so everyone remains on speaking terms. For Picasso, he convinces the other tenants that monkeys and turtles should be allowed to roam the hallways. For Nijinsky, he tries to convince Diaghilev that his prodigy is loyal. For the war, he develops reconnaissance photos in a brewery.

I predict that Steichen will continue to do things for other people for many years. When he returns to America, he will probably return to portrait and fashion photography. But one day, when he is middle-aged and begins to see his brief life slipping away from him, he will decide that he is fed up with doing things for others. He will drop everything and everyone and become utterly selfish. He will even get divorced. Then he will do his best work. Something utterly his own. And people will stand in awe of it and say, That—that is art. In this way, he will prove that photography is art. This has not yet been proven. But we will call it art here for discussion's sake.

Steichen is the ultimate representative of his art form. He is a persuasive spokesman for art photography. He defends the right of its practitioners to employ silhouettes, blurredness, accidents, and technical modifications in order to further their art. He avidly supports the notions that photographs should be exhibited as fine art, and that painters should not dominate the juries of photographic salons. He is a pioneer of color photography and of color photography as art.

But Steichen is also smart enough to know when to remain silent. He has not said anything about the feud between Stieglitz and Day, or the expulsion of Gertrude Kasebier and Max Weber from the Photo-Secessionists.

Stieglitz made Steichen possible. Steichen knows this. Steichen's genius lies in his ability to get what he wants out of people and landscapes. To do this, he must know what he wants and how to get it. Eventually, Steichen will be forced to break with Stieglitz, but by the time he does, he will no longer need Stieglitz, and Stieglitz will no longer be able to hurt Steichen's career.

Steichen knows color. Despite his willfulness, Steichen has no ill intentions. There are no outside impediments to Steichen's working successfully within the photographic art community. He was welcomed and praised there from his very first salon submission and was hailed as important by older men in his profession. In the art world this would be highly suspect, but in photography it is not.

Steichen's only stumbling blocks are the lure of commercial portrait photography and the rejection of photography's claim to be fine art—but even there he has supporters in Rodin, Shaw, and Maeterlinck. Steichen is a good painter, but painting no longer lures him.

Steichen organized all the shows of the Hôtel Biron artists at the 291 Gallery in America. In this way, Steichen has brought the art of the tenants of the Hôtel Biron to the Americans, although Steichen himself is not really an American. He was born in Luxembourg. But no one knows this.

Steichen admits that he has no idea what the name Photo-Secessionist means, even though he is one.

PABLO PICASSO

Picasso is Spanish. He started Cubism. He is perfectly willing to admit that he has no idea what he's doing. It's everyone else who is afraid to admit it.

Our quarrel is overrated. I am simply his nemesis. He wishes he understood color as well as I do, but won't admit it. We have split art in two, and each is carrying it in his own direction. He resents me for this, but it is for the best. Neither will be more important than the other.

Picasso has not yet learned how to stop working. He will have to learn. He is lavish in everything—food, women, work. Yet this is not a yearning to annihilate himself, as some say, but to make himself.

Since Picasso creates fashions instead of following them, he can risk being unfashionable. He can throw a party for Rousseau. He can design the sets for *Parade*. He is willing to move on, to regroup, to take risks.

As a result, there are periods in Picasso's art. Already people want to claim that some are more important than others, that the periods before the *Demoiselles* and since his new pastoral painting are less important than his Cubism. They are not. His periods aren't separable from each other. They are stops on a journey. The journey is important, not the stops.

What is his art to Picasso? Research. Just that. Only that.

Likewise, the current woman in Picasso's life represents the period he is going through. With women, as with art, Picasso is looking for something he will never find. He knows this, and he knows the point is to keep on looking. Critics are wrong when they say that Picasso's hatred of women is evident in his paintings of them. Picasso's paintings of women aren't about women. They are about art. Picasso's eroticism is already evident in his Cubist paintings, but no one will notice it for a long time.

Picasso is affected by his surroundings. His paintings change whenever he changes his studio in Paris or his summer home in the country. Picasso was not affected by his sudden wealth or fame, but like everyone he is profoundly affected by the War. Despite the War, he is very young to have had so many close friends and lovers die. Since childhood, Picasso lives in a constant state of mingled grief and revelry, as if he were always at a wake. The War has ruined everything for now, and it will ruin some artists permanently, but it will not ruin Picasso.

Picasso will not give titles to his paintings, and yet he creates new names for the women he lives with. Picasso's Eva is dead but, even so, what do Fernande, Eva, and Olga have in common? Their future without Picasso.

As willful as Picasso seems to other people, he lets his art rule him. It is the only thing he allows to rule him.

Almost all artists suffer at one time or another with indigestion and trouble with the law. Picasso has already experienced both of these.

Many artists lack confidence. Picasso does not. He doubts his work, but he never doubts himself.

Picasso is not afraid of otherness. All his friends are poets.

ERIK SATIE

Everyone agrees that Satie is the most insulted, derided, and ridiculed composer of the age. But they also agree that he is oversensitive.

Everyone says that Debussy was Satie's greatest friend. Debussy allowed Satie to dine with him but made him drink inferior wine. Satie wanted to adapt a Maeterlinck play, and Debussy thought it was such a good idea that he obtained permission for himself before Satie could even ask. Debussy could have introduced Satie's music to the public but chose not to. When Ravel finally did so, Debussy was angry and surprised that anyone actually liked it.

Satie's irony does not mask his bitterness. It often vents his bitterness. And when he is whimsical and puckish, he is not hiding anything. He sees the world that way. Are people of Honfleur who are born of Scottish mothers never puckish? Why can't people be who they are? Why must they be protecting themselves?

Satie is a fetishist. He could not be without some form of affectation. Satie's personal eccentricities extend much farther than his dress. Instead of bathing, he scrapes himself with a pumice stone. Weekly, assiduously, he sends all his collars and handkerchiefs out to be laundered, but he will not clean his room or hire anyone to do it. He likes to carry lit pipes and hammers in his pockets, since the umbrella is always on his arm. He hates the sun and stays up all night. No one understands Satie. Satie is the only one who doesn't try.

Satie does nothing but write. He sits in cafés and composes music in sets of threes, using different colored inks, writing in a calligraphic hand and including copious marginal directions to the musicians, which he believes are essential to the piece but forbids to be read aloud during a performance. He also invents ideas for music that he never composes, and writes the ideas down in his notebook.

Anyone who goes back to school at forty is either courageous or humiliated. Satie was both. He wanted to improve his music and become known for his new innovations. Instead, he has improved his music and become known for his old innovations. He pretended to be bitter about this but was secretly flattered, and he wrote more during that time of flattery than he did before or has since. This proves that the artist is too susceptible to discouragement and encouragement alike. These are obviously dangerous things and should be avoided at all costs.

The reason Satie's new music is not recognized is that one is not permitted to change one's character in France. Therefore, he was not really permitted to go back to school and write different music, even though he did it anyway.

Furniture music is the music of the future, but no one

knows it. *Socrates* is Satie's best work so far, but no one realizes it. Satie is the only artist I know whose work continues to flourish during the War, but no one will admit it.

Twenty years ago Satie moved to the suburbs, and except for his room here in the Hôtel Biron, he has lived there ever since. Satie prefers the gloom of the suburbs to Paris, and I have no idea why he condescends to loiter with us painters. He confessed to me that he learns more about music from painters, but he may have been flattering me.

Satie is childlike, but he is not a primitive and should not be compared to Rousseau, though he often is. Satie is childlike and shrewd; Rousseau was never shrewd. Satie should not be compared to anyone.

No one likes Satie's music because they are afraid that he is playing a joke on them and that he will get the last laugh. Satie's music is no joke.

If Satie hadn't played the piano at the Chat Noir and Auberge du Clou, he would never have had a mistress. He is afraid that if he were ever comfortable, his music would no longer be any good. That is why he refuses to live with a woman, or have his room cleaned, or accept large sums for his music to be published. The idea that he might be cuckolded, or that women don't understand him, is rubbish.

Socrates is Satie's only humorless work. I already said that it may be his best. He could not have written it until Debussy died. Satie is a miniaturist in music. His triptychs are three-sided, sculptural music. He insists on spareness because he is tired of this Decadence and Romanticism and German music, even though he was against the ban on German music when the War started.

Satie is the only artist I know who has successfully avoided ordinary life. He lives in a world of his own construction.

Satie happened in France. He could not have happened in any other country.

VASLAV NIJINSKY

People like to say that Nijinsky is only emotional, only instinctual, only physical, only intuitive, that he is really an animal or a creature from another world. This is untrue. Nijinsky can only express himself through motion.

Everyone is so thrilled because, when Nijinsky leaps, he pauses for a moment in the air before coming down. In the future, Nijinsky's secret method will be revealed, and all the dancers and athletes will be required to learn it.

What should thrill people are his choreography, his ingenuity of movement, his ability to transform himself into the character. Of course, these things don't.

No one appreciates Nijinsky's choreography—it is too modern for the moderns, more advanced than any other art form. The most scandalous and innovative of his dance movements have been improvised. They have come directly from the character Nijinsky has allowed to overwhelm him. The only reason *Afternoon of a Faun* was so shocking was because no one could deny that, for a moment, Nijinsky became the Faun.

Like the painters here at the Hôtel Biron, Nijinsky hates prettiness. His choreography shows that. Nijinsky becomes the music when he dances and wants his audiences to understand his ballets as much by their physicality as their choreography. Nijinsky is looking for something beyond prettiness—what we are all looking for.

The public is fascinated by the strength of Nijinsky's legs, but his real power is in his abdomen. This is why Rodin loved him. There is no power in the extremities.

In this period of showy decadence, Nijinsky is the only performing artist who is truly erotic. This is another reason why he is profoundly disturbing, and yet another reason why Rodin loved him.

Nijinsky is aware of the tension between the Greek and Egyptian, and used it in *The Rite of Spring*. Nijinsky insisted on preserving his childlikeness and innocence because he knew it was essential to his art. Nijinsky's work is perfect because he has achieved a synthesis of his nature and his training.

Geniuses who are able to abandon themselves can be controlled. They never know when to accept protection and when to fight it. When Nijinsky was well, he protected his mother and sister vehemently but did not know how to protect himself. After Diaghilev threw him out, Nijinsky tried to start his own company and manage his business affairs, but he is only a genius at dance and choreography. We like to think it is bad luck that the first person he finds—Diaghilev—will not let him flourish and then destroys him. We would like to think it is bad luck that he cannot manage his own business affairs and cannot find anyone else after Diaghilev to do it.

Diaghilev and his dancers did not destroy Nijinsky because he left Diaghilev and married a woman. They destroyed him because he is the best dancer—not of their time, or up until this day. Nijinsky is the best dancer ever. They realized this and so they destroyed him. It is easy to destroy genius. There is no glory in it.

Nijinsky did not go mad because Diaghilev rejected him. Nijinsky went mad because, after Diaghilev, he could not find another opportunity to dance and choreograph. And so his heart died. You cannot live through a war like this one when your heart has died.

You may blame Diaghilev if you like. He was the instrument of Nijinsky's destiny. Nijinsky was incapable of making his way alone. Someone else might have enabled him to dance a full twelve years instead of only six, and to choreograph and teach another fifty. Or someone might have come along who could not help Nijinsky at all, and only the Russians would have known about him. We cannot know who the others might have been. What we know is that Nijinsky danced for six years and choreographed for only two. His is the only real tragedy at the Hôtel Biron.

Nijinsky is at home in the water. He loves weightlessness. He seeks oblivion. Don't we all.

RAINER MARIA RILKE

Another word for Rilke is longing. He longs to write but has extended periods when he produces nothing. He longs to be loved by a woman in a particular way but cannot determine what that way is. He longs to love the way a woman loves but feels that men are inferior at love, and this prevents him. He longs to be understood, but that is too much to ask.

To Rilke, no one is ever pure enough, right enough. He applies these standards to his own work. This overly critical sense prevents him from working. It forces him to suffer long intervals when he tries but cannot work. He repeatedly tortures himself about his inability to work. He finally succumbs to exhaustion. He sleeps. He wakes up refreshed. In an access of gratitude, unself-consciously, he falls into a swoon and writes, without stopping, an immortal work of literature.

Rilke has made his pilgrimage to Italy for the sake of Burne-Jones and Rossetti. It is rumored that, when in Venice, Rilke wears a black-and-red-striped bathing costume.

Rilke believes that he is a Carinthian. He believes that everything originates in the blood. Most exiles who travel aimlessly and have no country feel compelled to invent their origins and create elaborate personalities based on them, as if this excused their odd behavior. These are displaced persons, and you should pay no attention to their particular style of mythmaking.

Rilke is especially fond of women, children, and animals, because they rely on their intuition. He wants to make childhood into a cult and childlikeness a necessity for grownups. He trusts his own intuition. He sees the world as divided into the childlike and the grownup. The Germans, of course, are grown up. This he finds a sign of their stupidity.

Rilke travels to get away from himself, not to find himself. Rilke is always trying to get away from himself. But when he travels, he is looking for a way to work. Rilke is a procrastinator. He will do his best work when he knows he is about to die.

Paris is the closest thing that Rilke has ever had to a relationship. Paris attracts and repels him. He tries to get away but comes back. He will always come back. Paris is his good woman. Nothing is as interesting or as painful to Rilke as Paris, except perhaps himself.

Rilke subsists on a monthly income from his German publisher, Anton Kippenberg, and from an anonymous Austrian donor, who is a woman. All Rilke's great friends are women. Rilke is one of the few artists in Paris who truly values women and wants them to be as interesting and powerful as he is. Women are drawn to him, and he needs a fascinating woman nearby at all times. But when she gets too close, he withdraws. For Rilke, withdrawal is a creative act.

Rilke admires women so much that he has studied the ones throughout history who have been unlucky in love. He has translated their letters, memoirs, and poetry. He envies them their ability to love so completely and their ability to suffer from it. Rilke would like to make the love of women a religion like other religions.

Everybody praises Rilke's *The Notebooks of Malte Laurids Brigge* for its evocation of Paris. No one even notices that it is the most apt treatise since Shakespeare on the difference between being loved and loving.

Rilke reads memoirs, chronicles, letters, searching for evidence to substantiate his views on love. He is interested in the romances of artists like the Brownings because he hopes that romantic love between two artists is possible. He is more interested in an artist's personal life than in his art, as if looking for keys to his own life and, through that, for a key to his art. Rilke has no personal life. He is not capable of it.

Rilke has sought out great artists to admire, but his obsessions last only long enough to answer his immediate questions. With Tolstoy the question was, Must one be an artist? With Rodin it was, How do I live? With Cézanne, How do I reconcile the intuitive with the intellectual? And with Gide, How do I reconcile life and art? Now that Rilke has found partial answers to all these questions, he may not have the need for a great artist in his life again and may never acquire another love of this kind.

Rilke is demoralized by the War and, to console himself, is studying astronomy. He feels he is poorly educated; as a result, he approaches everything as a beginner.

Rilke believes in the voluptuous soul and understands the painterly idea of the body as landscape. Of all the writers in Paris, he is one of the few who understands the correspondences among the arts, respects the visual arts, and uses concepts drawn from the visual arts for his own work.

Rilke has participated in séances where spirits have been willing to speak irreverently through him, waging vendettas and engaging in inane monologues.

Rilke likes to read ladies' fashion journals and has fallen in love with actresses. Art is more real to him than life. Rilke's greatest struggle is to reconcile life and work. So far, he has failed. Rodin's old age was a great disappointment to Rilke because it lacked dignity.

Rilke is only attracted to people he hopes might understand him. The only thing that matters to Rilke is the life of the emotions. Rilke makes you see through his eyes.

JEAN COCTEAU

I could write: The Brief Life of Cocteau, Number One; The Brief Life of Cocteau, Number Two; The Brief Life of Cocteau, Number Three; etc. They would all be different. They would all be true.

Cocteau adores other people with a headlong abandon that is typical of impetuous youth. But he is no longer a youth. He will retain this childlike quality into old age and complain that he is still too young.

Cocteau prefers to love men who are reluctant parties. He used to love men much older than himself; but now that he is approaching thirty, he has begun to love boys. Cocteau will provide all the love and guidance for these boys that he wanted when he himself was a boy. Of course, they won't want it.

Cocteau has been accused of being a dilletante and a dandy rather than a serious artist. But he will be a serious artist one day. His most impressive contribution to art so far is his organization of the event called *Parade*, in which he induced Picasso and Satie to collaborate. I imagine that Cocteau's real genius will be revealed in his old age—in some masterpiece of staging, in some collaborative effort, perhaps in some ultra-modern field of art that has yet to be invented.

It would not be fair to say that Cocteau enjoys suffering. No one enjoys suffering. But suffering has become a habit with him, and he craves it the way he craves love. And I'm afraid that Cocteau might be prey to other addictions besides love.

An artist should not expect to be understood, but many do, and Cocteau is already one of these. I am afraid that, as a result, he will become bitter and resentful. Bitterness and hatred spell ruin for the artist.

We are all searching for something: I am searching for oblivion; Cocteau is searching for himself.

Cocteau is so colorful in his speech and gestures that he has already appeared as a character in one of his more famous colleagues' novels. I fear that, like the Count de Montesquiou, he will appear in many more of his colleagues' novels.

Cocteau claims that his artistic collaborators at the Hôtel Biron are his friends. They claim they are not. They will probably continue to collaborate over the years, and continue to bicker over whether or not they are friends.

Cocteau is one of the few Parisians at the Hôtel Biron. He marvels at how so many foreigners can reap so much artistic indulgence, inspiration, fame, and glory from his native city. Secretly, he envies them.

Cocteau sees the artistic world divided between Romanticism and Classicism. He has just abandoned the former to join the latter, and is now urging his friends to do likewise.

Like many artists, Cocteau feels lonely and insecure, and

will probably always feel that way. His morbid desire to please may be his way of showing how much he fears this.

Cocteau is prone to nervous diseases and suffers from eczema. Cocteau does his best work under the influence of romantic love. This will be both his glory and his downfall. Cocteau has no friends, only lovers. He wants sons, and will try to make them of his lovers.

HENRI MATISSE

I am not afraid to use my intuition. I use it all the time and for everything. I have been working very hard throughout the War and I am about to change directions entirely. My wish is about to be fulfilled.

I refuse to develop the bitterness I see destroy other artists. I am what I am. That is enough. In my art I seek oblivion in its various forms—oblivion, the thing without limits.

My use of color is never arbitrary. It is designed to make us see objects and their relation to each other in a new way. It is designed to bring out the heart—mine, yours, the one of the canvas.

Only Steichen understands my use of color. I am indebted to him even though I disapprove of photography.

Simplicity is not a choice. It is my direction. I have no choices, I have only to be diligent and follow my direction. No one else is going in my direction.

I travel to get away. Illness is a place I have traveled to before and will again. My family is a solace to me. I just want to understand myself.

Fauvism is the critics' way of explaining the incomprehensible but inevitable next step. I understand Cézanne better than anyone. I am a purist but I am never decorative. Deny the effect my painting has on you. Color, purity, bliss. Everything that is happening to me is happening right now.

I do not paint my desire but the quality of my desire.

Why am I telling you all this? Shall I go on?

Letters Not Sent: The Letters of Camille Claudel to Auguste Rodin

Monsieur Rodin,

I write to you now, when we have only just met, because in the moment of our acquaintance, I envision a time when I will be apart from you and unable to tell you my thoughts.

But I would not write to you at all if I planned to give you these letters. Of course not. How absurd. In the first place, you would throw them away. (You see how, even after our first meeting, I begin to know your wiles.) In the second place, I do not reveal my thoughts to my brother or closest friends, let alone to a complete stranger who has assumed the responsibilities of my real teacher, Alfred Boucher, who voyages to Italy.

Perhaps one day, if you prove to be extremely kind to me, I will let you read these letters, but then only in my presence, and only to prove to you that I was right. They will remain mine. They will be a testimony to what shall come. They will serve as a sort of prophecy.

I wish you hadn't left for London after we had just been introduced. I miss you. It seems all the more poignant now than if we were already friends. I am not a patient person.

Everyone discusses you here because of your piece *The Creation* in the Salon and your commission for the colossal doors for the Museum of Decorative Arts. I wish I had met you two years ago, before you had received the commission and the emphatic reviews from critics at the Salon, before people had begun to notice you, so I could have seen what you were like when you were still unrecognized. But two years ago I was only fourteen, a girl from the provinces (I still have my accent, as you remarked), and even though I was already studying with Monsieur Boucher, you would have thought me a child. I also wish we knew each other better because then, for example, you would post me letters filled with news of your adventures.

I wonder who tends your studio while you are away and wish that it were me. I am very organized.

1 8 8 1

Monsieur Rodin,

I am relieved that you have returned to Paris safely, and that I might now get to know you. I love listening to your stories of London, especially the ones about the museums and the Elgin Marbles, which you seem to admire so much. I am also happy that you have acquired a new student on the trip, the American Monsieur Natorp, who lives in London when he is not here studying with you. I know that he will pay you well, as I and the English girls cannot. You need the money. Just because you have a new commission and the critics have stopped slandering you does not mean that you can cover your expenses. I understand this.

I am also pleased that you have been asked to fashion more busts, and that Monsieur Legros will arrive in December to sit for one, because I know you need the money. But I must admit that I begrudge the time you will spend away from me and the English girls.

I am not jealous of the time you spend at work on the colossal doors because I know you are creating art. If I ever fell in love with you, I would have to watch you work because I would love you as much for that as for who you are when you're with me.

Since you will be visiting our studio to comment on our work, and we may even grow to be friends, perhaps I should tell you more about myself.

I have been sculpting since I was four. Do not ridicule me, sir, it's true. I have been carving marble since I was ten, and I engage one of our maids, Eugénie, to rough out the blocks for me. I have been studying with Alfred Boucher since I was thirteen. Under his tutelage I have completed busts of Bismarck and Napoleon, completed a figure that Monsieur Boucher named *David and Goliath*, and many groups of figures, some drawn from ideas in the poems of Ossian, much the way you have chosen Dante's *Inferno* as the inspiration for your colossal doors.

When I decided that I must follow my profession as a sculptor to Paris, my mother, sister, and brother felt obliged to accompany me. I am afraid that my family does not like me very much because they feel that they are forced to make compromises for my art. I was willing to venture out alone, but my mother forbade it. Here in Paris (and already in Soissons) they feel crowded because my work occupies so much space. My younger brother complains that I tyrannize his boyhood. I think he envies me. They all condemn art. My mother and sister feel utterly that the artist's profession is amoral, and so they fear for my chastity. My brother believes that the artist's life is far too messy—what with clumps of clay, chunks of plaster and wax, and stone chips collecting in layers of dust everywhere. He also objects to the messiness of the works of art being produced in our time. He says that they are gross and ugly, products of vice and sloth.

Since they oppose my calling so strongly, you must wonder why they followed me to Paris. They should have been happy to see me take my "mess" away to the city. I believe they came for three reasons. First, in the provinces they grew accustomed to their martyrdom for the sake of Art, and now they are reluctant to abandon it. Second, they sense, in spite of themselves, a meaning in my pursuit of art, and they would feel empty without it. Finally, I believe my sister and mother are sincere in their concern for my reputation and hope to save my chastity by accompanying me.

You wonder how I can proceed in the face of so much opposition. But I suppose you know that for me, like you, art is not a choice, it is a calling. I never doubted what I would do in life, I never considered any other occupation. I have always felt I was born to sculpt, that my whole being was styled to this enterprise. At sixteen I have acquired the skills I need.

I don't know that I could prevail if my entire family were

against me. But my father has always loved me and understood my destiny. He has not made life difficult for me. He holds the rest of the family at bay.

You will think me domineering because of the way I've organized my group of English sculptresses, chosen our studio and models, invented their poses, divided up the chores, and arranged for the collection of rent. I have no family money for my training here in Paris, so I must devise a set of circumstances in which I can pay my own way. The English girls are not in their own country; they are timid about taking the initiative and making decisions. Like you, I might be shy or indifferent when it comes to social or family life, but for anything that has to do with art, I have plenty of initiative and I am not afraid to order people about.

1 8 8 1

Monsieur Rodin,

You ask me if it bothers me that sometimes you conduct yourself like my younger brother. Of course not. It is only natural, since you had an older sister you loved so much and I have a younger brother I love very much. It's true that I am only sixteen and you are forty, and that the separation in our ages might make this liaison seem absurd to others, but who cares about the others? What do they know about us?

I was very moved that you confided to me the secret of your sister. I understand why you have been unable to love a woman so completely again. But you seek my approval in this, and even though I respect and admire you, and am touched by your confession, I cannot consent. I don't believe a person should promise another not to love. However grievous the sin, that is too much to exact for penance. If you are still so desolated by the loss that you cannot love, I can sympathize deeply, sir, and offer you all the comfort and tenderness I have to give. But if you choose not to love, I cannot approve. You kill yourself by half measures, and you impede the true expression of your art if you refuse to let yourself feel deeply. I believe that emphatically. But I do not think you pathetic when you entreat me in your childlike way, like a younger brother. I receive it as a token of friendship, and I cherish it in much the same way as I cherish you.

You mustn't mistake my pride for heartlessness. I have cultivated it as a way to succeed in the face of my family's opposition. I am capable of love. I am not brittle. Surely you must see that. I am thrilled that you showed me your initial drawings after Dante. To have passed a whole year at nothing but that! I did not count on you being so singular of purpose. What a black, evil world to have inhabited so long. You frighten me now—to think that from Dante's *Inferno* your mind could conjure up such images!

You had reason not to utilize these sketches for the doors, and instead to model from real figures to see what might result. But certainly, the year was not lost, because you would not have been able to imbue these new figures with the sense of torment, of anguish, of despair, and especially of longing, if you had not spent that year in hell yourself.

It is ridiculous to say that I inspire the longing and desire in the new figures for your colossal doors. You barely know me—longing is for someone lost who cannot be recaptured, not for what might someday be.

I liked our walk to the Church of the Madeleine yesterday afternoon. Perhaps I just like to walk with you. I miss the walks with my brother that we took when we lived in the country. I would like to walk with you in the countryside, but even our trip a few blocks to the Madeleine was an adventure for me. With you everything is an adventure because I see everything with new eyes, as if the world I have been living in for so long had been transformed all at once and become more intimate.

You have reason to glean from the Madeleine that your colossal doors would be improved by abandoning the separate panels, employing figures that are almost whole, and adding some freestanding figures. I think that you discovered this beforehand, and the Madeleine just confirmed what you already knew. Of course, you must demand more money and the Ministry must approve. It is all very tiresome. I myself don't understand how you can bear to execute commissions and at the same time create art. But you do, and in this case you need the extra funds.

1 8 8 2

Monsieur Rodin,

Let us correct one thing right now, sir, if you are to be my new teacher. The remark your colleague Monsieur Dubois made—about my work owing something to yours—is not only false, it is erroneous. I assure you that when he made the remark to me, I had never even heard of you. He did it to compliment you, because he feels sorry for you, and rightly so, on account of the false accusations of *surmoulage* made against you. And yes, perhaps he saw slight similarities in our work— we do have things in common, you and I, make no mistake. But I have found my secrets in the Florentines; I am not ashamed of it. You have found yours in Michelangelo. That is the fundamental difference between us and always will be. So do not flatter yourself by believing Monsieur Dubois said he thought I had already studied with you. He simply phrased his remark in that way to impress upon my real teacher, Alfred Boucher, who was also present, that he might safely put me into your hands while he was voyaging in Italy.

Do not misunderstand me. This is not to say that I don't respect your work, or that I don't have anything to learn from you. I do. Only a student lacking in confidence would be afraid to admit that. You have great talent and mastery and even genius, and I, your very first student, will learn many things from you, I'm sure. But my work does not resemble yours and never will. I will be your student, but do not try to make me your disciple. Do not try to cast a shadow over my art in order to diminish its importance. History has proven that one great artist can study with another. You had no teacher because you did not have the confidence to be able to learn from one and still hold on to your own truth. I do. But if you insist that your students live in history under your shadow, I will leave you.

Do not try it. I know you have these ideas because you are jealous, because my work was exhibited and reviewed in the newspapers by the time I was fifteen, and you are only now getting exhibited and reviewed at the age of forty. My brother is also jealous; already at his young age I see him conspiring to be a greater writer than I am a sculptress. He does not seem to understand that both brother and sister can be great. But I will not let him subjugate me, and I will not let you.

No, of course I don't think it's wrong of you to seek out an audience with Hugo, and to obtain permission to do his bust. Of course it would be an honor and it would be an important work. I complain of the busts only because I feel you want too much to be a part of Parisian society and are willing to sacrifice your art to it.

And no, I do not think you were wrong in inviting the journalist Bazire to your studio, even if it was a way to obtain an introduction to Hugo. I do think it was unkind of you to call Bazire's festival in Hugo's honor a rehearsal for his funeral, even though you may have been right in saying so.

Pursue what you will within the realm of art. You don't need my approval in all things, though I'm flattered that you seek it. After all, we barely know each other.

1882

Rodin,

I am afraid that I'm falling in love with you. What makes me more afraid is that you might be falling in love with me. I like and dislike these ideas for several reasons.

I have never been in love before. Not truly, like this. It strikes me as the culmination of something I have been striving for in my art. I am not sure yet what that means, but that is the way it feels. Everything is so heightened. Everything matters. When you brush against me, or I feel your breath against my neck, it gives me the strangest sensation, as if my whole body were filling up and every muscle had contracted.

It makes my senses more acute, makes me notice things I wouldn't otherwise. I watch you move, watch your eyes, watch you blink, watch your expression change.

Even at a distance, this love gives me pleasure. I am thrilled to watch your work develop. Your ideas grow more sophisticated, you change and adapt them, you use what you know, you bring such intensity to the process. I am learning in a different way now. Even art has been brought to a sweeter level. I am so young, I am afraid I do not explain these things with enough precision.

I worry about this love because of the promise you made to your sister. Will you be able to love completely? Will you want to? Will you choose to? It seems only natural that we, two great artists who are about to become recognized, should work together and fall in love. But I am afraid that you are not willing. And I worry because I see very clearly that you are trying to make me jealous with the attentions you pay my companion and your student, Jessie Lipscomb. But it is you who are deceived. Jessie is English. The English are rarely swayed by false flattery. She realizes that it is me you are falling in love with. She first brought it up to me. I did not even have to call it to her attention.

So Jessie will not fall into your plan. You will not be able to use her complicity to make me jealous. She will remain loyal to me. You will have to admit sooner or later that you are falling in love with me, so you might as well do it now. Your tricks will not work anyway. And, if you must be told, sir (since you do not seem to be catching on), even though I am proud and confident and a great artist, and see through your ploys to win me by trying to hurt me, this does not mean that I am incapable of love. On the contrary, I can love you because I am confident, because I am proud, because I see through your ploys, and because I am a great artist. If I were not, I would be in great danger since you, like my brother, try to hurt me.

So you need not try to play with me because you fear I will not love you. That is nonsense. But if you fear an equal both in love and art, if you fear the truth, then I cannot help you with that, can I?

1 8 8 2

Rodin,

No, I am not sorry we made love. If I were going to be sorry, I would not have done it.

You needn't fear for my chastity. No artist has a chaste heart; that is what my family fears. I am a passionate person, like you. A tender person, like you. And like you, I have never felt quite this way before.

I understand how unhappy you must feel, but please do not despair. You should not be surprised that the master of literature, Victor Hugo, is really a cranky, tyrannical old man, who refuses to pose for you and is suspicious because some third-rate sculptor modeled an inferior bust of him ten years ago. At least he has consented to let you roam about the house and be near him. Certainly, with your great ambition and fierce will, you can find ways to draw closer to him, and to observe him from all the necessary angles. Perhaps you will need to sketch him now, even though this goes against your new sensibilities.

Please do not give up, my little wise man. You will prevail.

1 8 8 3

Rodin,

You needn't have been so anxious about Ballu's visit. I know he was one of those who several years ago made the charge of *surmoulage* against you, and so you had cause. But none of them could make a charge against you now without arousing a storm of public protest. They must all be ashamed of that mistake by now. And so they are forced to look at your work anew.

Of course, he cannot free himself from all his reservations.

71

Surely you must have anticipated that. I know that you are so absorbed in your work, it is as though you labored from inside it and saw it only from that perspective. So you have a tendency to forget that, to an outsider, this work is strange and unprecedented. It is natural for a man like Monsieur Ballu, who betrays his lack of confidence by his suspicion, to cite minor details, such as his inability to see the small figures mounted on the doors.

Don't exaggerate so. On the whole his report was good (at least he recognized the anguish in the figures), and you already have the additional monies you requested. You can go on working. Let this be enough for you this time, you who are never satisfied.

I do not enjoy the time you are away from me and at the great Monsieur Hugo's, but I admire how you persist. And no, I don't think you wrong in enlisting the help of Hugo's maid, or his mistress, or his daughter, or whoever else is necessary to help you gain access to the great man. For art must be completed at all costs.

It is truly cunning the way you manage to have your place at the dinner table changed to suit whatever angle you need to gaze upon the great writer from that day, and the way you can draw so skillfully on those tiny cigarette papers without Hugo noticing. I'm surprised you have not lost even more weight than you have; I cannot imagine you getting a chance to eat anything at these bizarre sittings. I cannot imagine anyone, not even the Pope, being so difficult, sir, so I truly sympathize when you complain about how hard it is, and I don't think that you're becoming as cranky as he is. And even though I cannot be there with you, I am touched by the way you bring all the small incidents at his house back into the studio to tell me, in little asides while you work, as if you must relive the events to better shape the bust. But I am glad it is to me that you recount the story, and not to some other student or model or artisan. I want to believe that you love me.

1 8 8 3

Rodin,

You need not look at my move from my studio on the rue Notre Dame des Champs to yours on the rue de l'Université as your triumph over me. It is not. It is only natural, now that I am working with you, that I should want to work near you. Anyway, it is not as if I were living with you. I live with my family. And do not fool yourself: I do not belong to you. If I belong to anyone, it is to myself (and even that is in doubt, since above all I belong to my art) and perhaps a little to my father. Unlike you and my brother, my father is kind to me. He understands that I am seriously devoted to art, and he helps me as much as he can. He does not try to trick me or ruin me. I wish I loved only people like my father, but I have not met any other people like him. (Even my sister and mother are against my profession.)

I devote myself to art, not to you. I moved to your studio for my own reasons. I did not like feeling torn between the two places. I am not like you, who cannot make a commitment to one studio, or to one place of residence, or to one woman, or to your art. You have many studios, and it is not because your work is so voluminous. You have many places of residence, and it is not because you need a change of air and scenery. You have more than one woman, and it is not because one woman cannot fill your needs. You are at work on more than one sculpture at a time, and it is not because you have a vast creativity. This multiplicity (do not confuse it with abundance) persists in all facets of your life and art because you are unable to commit. You are frantic, running from house to house, woman to woman, studio to studio, sculpture to sculpture. You are running away from yourself, from your feelings, from your art. What would happen if you stopped to look at it, to feel it, to concentrate? I shudder to think of it. You might break your whole world apart and find something inside. What? That is the secret you hide from yourself.

I must admit that I enjoy making the hands and feet for your sculpture. It is a job for me, just the way you, in your earlier years (and sometimes still now), worked for Carrier-Belleuse and the others making vases and cornices and decorative cupids. It's an honest job, to support my art.

If I make the hands and feet in your style, it is not because I can only copy your style, but because it is my job and because I am a skilled craftsman who understands your work well, perhaps better than you would like me to.

So if it is just a job, and I copy you because I must, why do I like the hands and feet? There are many reasons, and I will not reveal all of them. But I will tell you this—I like them because they are small. My work is not like yours. While you create these colossal white doors and populate them with masses of figures, I do the opposite. In private, on my own time, I create tiny figures that I can lay in the palm of my hand. You do not appreciate them because you are too busy running away to understand what is precious. But these figures are the key to my art, and some day you will understand their secret genius. If you ever do understand, you will be filled with grief because you will be forced to admit that I became a great artist in my own right.

But the shaping of the hands and feet is good practice for me in developing my true art, the art of the miniature, if you will (which has not been tried in modern sculpture), the way fashioning vases and cupids and caryatids was good practice for you in developing your art.

But, in addition to practice, it is a joy to work with the hands and feet because of their special character. They are so expressive, as if the joy or grief or love of an entire human body could be expressed simply in the gesture of the hand or the curl of the toes.

You should not worry so much that I am quiet and absorbed when I work in your studio, and that I do not socialize with the others. I don't act this way because I am uncomfortable or because I feel you are a taskmaster who insists that we work without respite. I am simply absorbed in my work. By nature I am a very restless, passionate person, and as a result I find it hard to find peace. One of the reasons I love my profession so much is that when I concentrate on my art, I lose myself in it, and this dissipates my restlessness and gives me the peace I need.

Furthermore, it is silly to be worried about my working for you. I do not mind it. There is no shame in it. You had to work for others; even now you do an occasional vase for Sèvres. You worry too much about how I feel, and you misinterpret my pride. It causes you harm. I don't want that. It will make your dyspepsia and insomnia worse. I am flattered that you would confide these troubles to me, but now I worry about you and don't want to be the cause of them.

I would never actually tell you this because it might make you vain, but there is another reason I don't mind working for you. You will become the greatest sculptor of your time. Already the critics are beginning to sense it, as you set about to create your colossal doors. I am not threatened by genius, on the contrary, I thrive on it. It will make me a better artist. I will use you in this way. I hope you will not mind it.

1883

Rodin,

I am not surprised to learn that Hugo has been betraying his mistress with his maid; great men seize all the advantages, and most of them are at the expense of women.

I do not like this. You must know that. I do believe we should be free to love, men and women alike. Every young artist in Paris this decade believes it. But there is enough suffering in the world; why choose to inflict more? Why not be content to love one person and, in doing so, spare the feelings of others? I too am a passionate person; I understand how I could love more than one man. But if I insisted upon exercising that right, wouldn't I be causing all three of us torment? That is the part I could not do. For certainly, I could love another man (I admit I love you), but I could not torment us all by being another man's lover. Can't you understand that?

I do not like the way you examine my face when you give me this kind of news. It makes me think you are trying to look into the future. Perhaps you already have, at Monsieur Hugo's.

No, I do not mind posing for you. I do not feel it lessens me or cheapens me, or lowers my stature as an artist. On the contrary, I think that it helps me as an artist and that perhaps you have lost something as an artist by never having had the occasion to pose yourself. When I pose, I can see the artistic process from the other side; instead of looking at the object, I become the object. It is an interesting exercise. It is almost like two sides of the same experience—loving and being loved, for example. I do not think an artist should be without it. Perhaps I will ask you to pose for a bust, so you too can have the experience. An artist who does not pose is like a composer who never listens to music.

Also, I do not mind posing for you because I am not like the other models. You love me; you do not love them. I am an artist; they are not. And I especially do not mind because of the way you look at me so intensely, as if you craved the beauty of the female form more than any other man in the world. You hide this feeling under a mask of lechery because that is acceptable; but I know the true nature of your feeling.

Then, what is even more delightful is the way you look at me so closely, as if you understood what it is to be a woman, as if you'd imagined it so thoroughly that you'd crossed the line that God has made between us and become a woman yourself. That is why you like to make figures of two women in the act of love with each other—they are not really two women at all but rather you—so deeply ensconced in womanliness that for a moment you have become a woman yourself—making love to another woman. This to you would be the ultimate union, the ultimate merging, and to others, of course, it is the ultimate heresy, more unthinkable than Leda and the Swan.

I love the way you draw so close to me and, without touching me, examine my skin, your hands and lips remaining just a hair's length away from my body, so that the air between your hands and my skin becomes like a blanket covering me, warming me with the strangest sensation.

This is so delicious, almost better than making love. It is like the moment right before satisfaction, when you feel yourself filling up inside and you believe you are about to attain everything you have always wanted.

I wonder if other men could make a woman feel this way. I wonder if losing yourself and becoming a woman is as exciting for you as it is for the woman you're gazing at. I wonder if you even realize what you are doing. Perhaps you do, since you try to hide it in the manliness of your long beard and thick frame. The other models, whom you don't love, do not understand what you're about—which is why they're afraid of it and believe you when you pretend it is instead only lechery.

But I don't understand how you can make love to your models when you don't love them. Yes, of course, I can understand how you would have wanted to before, when you were dissatisfied at home. But now that you love me it seems superfluous. I can't imagine how it could be interesting to make love to someone you don't love when you can make love to someone you do love like you love me. I will not ask you about it; we would only argue. You would say that men are not like women, that men make love to attain a variety of different pleasures and therefore can make love to a variety of different women. Or you would say that you were more in love with Woman in general than with any particular one, and that to deny yourself Woman in deference to the one you love would be to deny yourself Life. Or you might say that even if you wanted to stop, you couldn't.

I doubt you would deny that you love me. I hope we are beyond that charade. But I doubt you would admit that you are trying to subjugate me by not acknowledging my rights as your beloved. If you did not sleep with the models, you would be granting me this equality. That is why you continue to sleep with them. That is why you continue to deny me my rightful place by your side and instead grant it to someone who is not even part of your artistic life.

Does your wife, Rose Beuret (whom you subjugate by not making your legal wife and by not allowing her to participate in your artistic life), know that you will never love anyone the way you love me? If she did, perhaps she would not want to stay with you.

You say you need your wife to take care of you, but that is not true. The cook prepares your meals, the housekeeper cleans and sews and mends, the apprentices keep your maquettes damp and your plasters safe. You need your wife because you need someone who is beneath you to submit to your selfish, cruel treatment.

But then you complain that she harangues you and torments you because you will not give her her way. Then you conclude that all women are shrews because men will not give them their way. Did it ever occur to you that you have made her a shrew? Yes, you, through your unjust treatment. If you cannot treat a woman with kindness, as an equal, and share your life with her, then you should not live with her and subject her to such torment. You claim she clings to you and will not leave. Maybe so. But it could not have been that way at first. She was young and beautiful once. She could have met a kind man who would have married her. But you occupied her. You had her model for you, keep your clay maquettes damp, take care of your affairs when you were away. And then you did not give her what was her right.

I would not have stayed with you if you had not treated me kindly and as an equal. Perhaps that is why you will not leave her. She will put up with your abuse, and you can complain that she has clung to you.

I do not envy her, but I do wish that I had met you when she did, twenty years ago, when you were young and frail, embarrassed and shy. Perhaps it would have been different between us. Perhaps you would have been able to give me the kindness and equality I require. But I wonder why I believe this, since you did not give it to Rose.

And then, you complain that I don't give you my heart. Look at all you have from me—don't you see it? Look at the figures you've made for the colossal white doors—don't you see the love of women, the bliss and torment? I do. And so many brilliant, usable figures all at once, when before it took you months to create one. And so many figures with my body, with my face. People will say I have benefited by our acquaintance, but it is you, sir, who reaps.

1 8 8 3

Rodin,

You should not have had such little confidence in Monsieur Ballu. You see how he is catching on and beginning to appreciate your colossal doors. You, who often tell me patience is a form of action, are too impatient—with the Ministry, with the public, with the critics, with other artists. Now that everyone is beginning to notice you, you should forget all your bitterness about the past. Saying you will forget it because you love me is pure silliness. You finally have the recognition and approval you are seeking, not just for the doors but for all your work, even that of the past. You might as well admit it.

I am touched by the way you have begun to consult me in all that you do. I know that you are a great artist with ideas of your own, but it pleases me that in addition to loving me, you also value me as an artist, and now you feel hesitant to act without knowing what I think. It is as though we were growing up together, you and I, through our love for each other and our art. I know you don't notice these things. I suppose you cannot admit them. But Jessie notices, and even your friend Monsieur Morhardt has spoken to me about it. So even if you can't admit it, you can't deny it.

1884

Rodin,

Another commission! Of course I am pleased that you have been chosen for the *Calais* monument. And since you asked, of course I don't think it's wrong that you want to portray more than one Burgher. Even if it wasn't what the committee had in mind and will cost more, you must do what your heart tells you to do. They have chosen you for your genius, not merely for your artisanship to sculpt the monument. In doing so, they choose to submit to your will in its conception and design. I believe in that truly.

Furthermore, I think it very diligent of you to do reading on your subject's history and to visit the locales where events took place. You make every effort to immerse yourself in your subject. Many sculptors would not take such pains, would not be willing to lose themselves in another time or place or personage the way that you are.

I am happy you are so satisfied with the first maquette. I have never seen you content with a sketch the way you are with this one. I know that you will make many studies and sketches before you are through, and that the work will go through many transformations. But I wonder if the process has become easier for you as a result of your having worked so assiduously on your colossal doors. You seem to have acquired an élan, an ease of execution that you didn't have before, as if some problem that had been troubling your mind had been resolved.

You are not wrong to ask certain friends who are close to the committee to speak to its members on behalf of your ideas. You must bring to bear whatever pressure you can and use whatever connections you have to do what is right.

Thank you for confessing to me how much you love me and exactly what I mean to you. To tell me that you have not felt this happy since Maria was alive, to tell me that it's the happiness of always being understood, of always having your expectations exceeded—this overwhelms me. I had no idea of the depth of your feelings.

Now I am ashamed of all the times I've yelled at you and complained about your treatment of me. But you must understand I could not have imagined that you felt this way. Yet, now that you tell me, it all seems right since I feel the same way about you, as if being with you was my destiny shaking my hand. Yet I am afraid, now that you have been so candid and tender, I will want you always to be so, though it appears you cannot. But perhaps this is untrue. Perhaps now that I know how you feel in your heart, I will not mind the things I minded before. I hope so.

1 8 8 4

Rodin,

I miss you and wish I could have traveled to Calais with you. At least I would be able to comfort you in the face of so much harsh criticism. I am sorry for what they said. Judging by your letter, it appears that they don't understand at all what you are trying to do. To say they are offended by the Burghers' dejected poses! To say they are insufficiently elegant and an offense to their religion! What an outrage! How do they expect a group of men to feel who are going off to be unjustly executed? I suppose they want from you what they are used to getting from Academy sculptors—the depiction of a false nobility that masks the true wretchedness of the moment. Well, don't give it to them. The time is over when sculptors give their figures' poses and expressions a syrupy coating like brandied cherries. I am surprised they do not realize this by now. Perhaps they would rather be reminded of the nobility of the act than of the moment's true horror, but that is no excuse.

I know it doesn't console you when I say that you have worked hard on this maquette and have done the right thing. But don't let them sway you.

1885

Rodin,

I am so pleased with my two figures being shown in the Salon that I did not mind when I read the catalog and found that I am listed as your student. I suppose, after all, I am and should not mind it, as long as I am not thought of that way much longer.

Are you satisfied with where the figures are placed? And with how the light hits them? I notice how you stand close to the figures as if you wanted to be near them. It has the effect of drawing people to them. I wonder if this is what you intend.

You also seem to be listening to what these others are saying as you stand there. Are their criticisms just? Is their praise fitting? And if their ideas seemed wrong-headed, would you intervene?

It never ceases to astound me how different figures look at an exhibition from the way they did in one's studio. At an exhibition you cannot help imagining you are all sorts of other people and looking at the figures through their eyes. How odd they look! How enigmatic! What mystery! And why that pose, why this expression? As you know, it is quite another matter altogether in the studio. I wonder where art would lead if the concerns of the critic and those of the public were identical to ours in the studio. Would that harmony allow us to explore unimpeded new ideas in art, or would that lack of tension make art deteriorate? It will never happen anyway, so I imagine there's no use pondering the question.

So what do you think of these two figures now that they are exhibited? I think they are a little too stiff. My brother's pride makes him look lifeless. The figure of Helen is almost too discerning, her gaze too precise.

I don't know. Remind me to ask you what you think. I don't know which is worse—not knowing what's wrong with a

figure in the first place, realizing what's wrong but not knowing how to fix it, or realizing what's wrong too late, when you
no longer have the heart to fix it. I suppose you postpone
indefinitely all these states of despair by never considering any
of your work finished.

1 8 8 6

Rodin,

I wish I had been present at Edmond de Goncourt's visit
to your studio. One hears so much of him. I would especially
like to know if he is as people say—perspicacious but petty.
There is no doubt that he is a very powerful man, but then, so
are you. I would have liked to see how he sized you up, how
he reacted to your figures.

I suppose that now you'll be invited to his Grenier meet-
ings, and of course you'll go. No amount of invitations from
influential people will be enough to satisfy your need for
respect. Instead, you should accept his solicitation of your
drypoints as a sign of respect. After all, he is a serious
collector.

You mustn't worry too much about the money for the
Calais monument. You have enough to worry about already of
things within your control. This is not. You can't help it, and
it's no reflection on you if the city has financial problems. The
monument will be cast and erected, all in good time. Try to be
patient.

1 8 8 6

Rodin,

This might truly be your moment of triumph. Last year
Dalou told the Ministry that your colossal doors might be the
most original work of the century, and now Mirbeau has written in *La France* that they are the most important work.

I know you understand the power of the press, since it was
you who taught me about it. And such praise coming from a

poet you admire! I am sure that now you feel as glorious as I do about your doors, as satisfied.

You should be quite proud, not simply to have gained the praise you have deserved for so long, but to have it shouted from the rooftops by one of France's most prestigious poets. Surely now you will be content. Why shouldn't you be?

I don't understand why you refuse to have the colossal doors cast in bronze. You have been given the money. Of course, you could work on them a little longer, make changes and improvements, but to what purpose? You could even go on working on the doors for the rest of your life, if you chose, never letting them out of your studio until you were dead.

I believe that is what you plan to do, but not so you can make improvements. You do it out of a meanness that is really selfishness. It is your usual persistence, carried to obsession. You want to hold on to everything that is dear to you—every lover, every woman you've possessed, every figure you've sculpted. You don't want to let anything go, you don't want anything to finish. That is a loss for you, not a triumph. It's the death of a part of you, and you fear that too many of these tiny deaths will eventually whittle you down to nothing.

Forgive me if I sound harsh, but I have just recognized this trait in you. I admit that I am still quite young and don't fully understand how the world works, so these discoveries stun me.

This whining of yours is ridiculous. I see right through it. You're being coy when you say that the doors remind you of me, and that if you're going to lose me, you won't relinquish the doors, which are your memory of me. First of all, you would not "relinquish" the doors by having them cast. You are simply unable to commit yourself to their final form. Second, if you really wanted to keep me, you'd be willing to give up those models you sleep with.

Furthermore, I don't like the idea that other artists are beginning to pay you visits because they have heard of your reputation as an eroticist as a result of your figures for the doors. I like to think of you as a sensualist, a man who loves the idea of Woman and perhaps one woman in particular, and indulges his senses and feelings to the fullest in these realms. But an eroticist is a collector of women, and I would not like to think of myself as part of a collection. I hope that this is not true and will never become so.

1 8 8 6

Monsieur Rodin,

You needn't try to turn the head of Jessie to get what you want from me. I will not write you any additional letters, we will not return to Paris any sooner, and Jessie will not extend to you any invitation to visit us in England. So your letters to Jessie are quite useless and do not make me in the least bit jealous. Furthermore, we do not think the reviews of your work in the newspapers that you send to us are the least bit ridiculous. We are quite content with them. What we do find silly is the way that you pretend you do not love me, pretend you are not preoccupied with me, pretend you are humble and meek and frank instead of stubborn and intractable and vain. In short, it is all these ruses that we find laughable, sir, not your art.

If you could grant me a little respect by admitting a bit more or, if you can't do that, by at least refraining from these naked ploys, perhaps we would want to return early from England. And what's more, you shouldn't write me such pathetic letters. I know that they're not sincere and that you're just trying to win me back—but on your own terms. What if I *have* come to England with Jessie just to get away from you? I don't deny it. I wish I could stay angry with you long enough to finally be rid of you. That is my finest wish to this hour.

I will tell you why I came away. When I first met you, I told myself that if you fell in love with me, you'd put things right between us, so I needn't worry. When you did finally love me but still didn't want to live with me or marry me, I thought you needed more time—perhaps to realize how much you loved me, or how different this love was from the way you'd felt before. I thought that maybe you needed to trust me more, to know that even though I am young and independent and have my art, I would be loyal to you and never leave you. So I gave you more time. And now I see that not only do you not plan to live with me or marry me or leave Rose (who would be happier without you), but now that you are famous, you are deceiving me with models and students and even visitors.

I finally see that it is not so much that you want me or Rose or any particular relationship or woman. You simply want to have your own way at all costs, and so whatever anyone else wants, you oppose.

That is why I have come away to England with Jessie, and none of your simpering, whining letters about how sad you are without me can disguise this fact of your nature. If you don't wish to change it, please do not keep sending these entreaties to Jessie and myself. You ask me to accept you on your own terms, but your terms are completely unreasonable. I will not do it. Please do not ask again.

1 8 8 6

Rodin,

I really wish you hadn't come here to the Lipscombs' to visit us. Wooton House was a peaceful, comforting place until you arrived. Your travel to London on business was a ruse I certainly saw through. It was underhanded to obtain an invitation from Jessie's parents by pretending to be gracious and posing as our longtime teacher.

I must admit your presence irks me a bit because it reminds me of how much I love you. I'm sure that's why you came. But none of your wiles, attentions, flatteries, or promises to obtain commissions for me will change my mind about things. What I want—a life and a home with you—you are too stubborn to give me. So now you must leave me alone. I won't yield to your tricks and entreaties.

1 8 8 6

Rodin,

I am glad you made a friend of Robert Louis Stevenson while you were in England. At least the trip was not wasted. It is good to have an artist friend from another country. That is the way I feel about Jessie. We have the same purpose, making art; but we have grown up with such different assumptions, different weathers, different languages, different foods, different views from our windows, different light and landscapes, that we go about our art in a different manner.

I'm sure it is the same way with your new friend. I know you admire literature and ideas, and you are flattered to have an eminent friend who writes you such beautifully phrased sentiments from so far away. I am embarrassed, though, to hear that you enjoy confiding in him. I would not like to think that a Scottish novelist knows about me and might paint an unflattering portrait of me in his book.

As far as your recent overdue commissions are concerned, I tried to warn you that you were spreading yourself too thin, but you would not listen to me. Your exuberance cannot be contained. Since this is so, you can do nothing more than keep working. At least it will keep you out of trouble with other women. You should not compromise your ideals by delivering figures before they are finished. If the committees must wait, then that is what they will do. Don't listen to their complaints and harangues.

You were right to exhibit this year at the Georges Petit Gallery instead of at the Salon. After all, you can't be everywhere at once. The Georges Petit is more prestigious this year, and you will get a much more sympathetic audience there for your *Eve* and *Crouching Woman* than at the Salon, whose audience simply would not understand.

1 8 8 7

Rodin,

No, I am not mad at you. I try to be angry with you, as you would see if you could read these letters, but it does not last long enough.

I understand why Jessie and Mlle Fawcett can no longer share a studio with me. They still want you to instruct them, and since I do not want to see you any more, you would be unable to visit them in the studio. I can surely understand how awkward it would be for all of us, and I certainly don't want to be reminded of you (you know how they talk about you) when I am trying so earnestly to forget you.

But I am sorry to lose my friends from the studio. It's not just a matter of expense. It will be so dreary without them. You must know (or perhaps you do not) how much I yearn for a group of artists, women artists, to work together and bolster each other in the face of the public's indifference and male artists' competitiveness.

But I suppose that now I will have more room and can therefore make a big mess as you do in your studio. Perhaps this will make me feel more important. Perhaps I will be able to work longer hours or concentrate more without the distraction of the other sculptresses—their projects, their needs, their banter. It may even be quite pleasant after all.

So don't think that I'm angry with you. I don't really want that, even though sometimes, when I am very hurt, I act as if I do. They say that you ask after me constantly and relay your invitations for me to come and work with all of you on Saturdays in your studio. I am reassured to know you have not forgotten me altogether, but please don't ask. It is so painful to try to forget about you. If you are sweet and kind to me, and ask me to forgive you, and invite me to work with you (which you know I love), then I'm afraid I will abandon all this unhappiness just to be with you again. But that will only make us both miserable after a time, as soon as you begin to deceive me again with other women.

I am not accusing you. I am just trying to explain to you why you please should not send me any more invitations or messages through Jessie or my other friends.

1 8 8 7

Rodin,

I don't want to criticize you, but I think you are spreading yourself too thin. I know you need to meet expenses, and so you feel obliged to take on more students from London, including the poet Browning's son. I know you feel that you need to accept commissions for busts of prominent people, especially since they have begun to approach you, and even commissions to decorate vases, beds, and sideboards as you have been doing recently.

But is it necessary to socialize with every poet, critic, and dignitary who invites you to his weekly breakfasts, Tuesday afternoon salons, and Saturday dinners? I thought you were a loner, like I am, and did not feel comfortable socializing with these people. I am not saying that you're incapable; I'm sure you could attend them as I could, act charming and make witty conversation. Even your timidity is winning. But shouldn't you devote this time to your art? Isn't enough time wasted in decorating furniture and fashioning busts for these people?

I'm afraid I don't understand this desire of yours to mix with society. I know you say you must, that you will not remain in the minds of the critics and ministers without socializing, and that without their approval you will not win future commissions, which in turn will bring you notice. Perhaps I am jealous, perhaps I want to be more important to you than these parties and dinners; but I also believe that the way to create great art is to spend time working at it, not socializing to secure your position. You say that I am idealistic in believing

VOICE: Lish?

LISH: Yeah?

VOICE: Lish at the Q?

LISH: Yeah.

VOICE: This is the plant.

LISH: The plant?

VOICE: The plant where you print your magazine.

LISH: Yeah?

VOICE: There's a problem.

LISH: Yeah?

VOICE: We're all set up to run and we see we've got no page ninety.

LISH: Oi gevalt.

VOICE: Yeah.

LISH: So what do we do?

VOICE: What do you want to do?

LISH: Oi gevalt.

VOICE: I'm waiting.

LISH: Jeez. God. Oh boy.

VOICE: So?

LISH: Gimme a sec.

VOICE: How about just make a clean breast of the whole thing?

LISH: A clean breast?

VOICE: Yeah, you know, explain, tell the truth.

LISH: The truth?

VOICE: Why not the truth?

LISH: But what about Marello? What about my mother?

VOICE: Come on, we'll just come clean. It's not a perfect world, you know?

LISH: What if we beg for mercy?

VOICE: That's it. A clean breast. Get down on your knees.

LISH: Just come right out with it and tell the truth?

VOICE: Not like Rodin. Like Lish. Be a man.

LISH: Oi, a man, a man. Please.

this. Perhaps you're right, perhaps I am young, provincial and naïve. But beyond jealousy and naïveté, it strikes me that something is truly wrong with this undertaking.

It is true that my brother has taken up with Mallarmé and his mob. He now admires Mallarmé the way he once did Rimbaud. Mallarmé, in his turn, admires my brother Paul and treats him as an equal. That is how it is among men. Paul will follow for a time, for he is only twenty. But when he does achieve stature, it will be on the terms as Mallarmé before him. Mallarmé will not assign him forever to student status.

It makes me wish that there were great bands of women artists, painters, sculptresses, who steadily pulled each other up into fame. But there are no such groups. You and my brother Paul and all the others like you won't allow it. Fame for each other, yes, as a form of protection. But not for us. And you tell me to beware of my bitterness, that it will ruin my art. But isn't it you who have made me bitter by keeping me always your student in the eyes of the world? Look at Paul, whose fame is now secured at the age of twenty, simply because the older poet has taken him under his wing. But you would not do the same for me. You did something that had the *appearance* of being the same but was really designed to ruin me. And then you reproach me for being bitter.

1 8 8 7

Rodin,

I have a confession to make. I thought I would not mind making it here since you will never read these letters, but even here I am embarrassed. I followed you to the model market this morning. I told myself I did not know why I wanted to follow you; I was not willing to admit the reason.

I wanted to see for myself how you looked at them, how you chose them. I knew that if I didn't feel jealous watching you there at the Place Pigalle, then I needn't be jealous of what I couldn't see.

91

Of course, the experiment failed. I was jealous. The girls are all so young. I know I am only twenty-three, but most of those girls are sixteen and none is over twenty.

And the way you looked at the most appealing ones, when they would lean against the fountain and appear preoccupied! You were so enticed by them; you were living a dream that had finally come true for you.

So I tried to end my jealousy, and instead I feel confirmed in it. I cannot forsake the memory I have of you, brushing up against those doe-eyed Italian girls who are only sixteen and promise you everything you've always wanted.

I know that most artists today make love to their models, that it's a practice widespread to the point of being commonplace, and that many artists consider it a necessary inspiration. But the way you cannot stop looking at a woman, the way you must possess her at that very moment with your eyes, makes me think that this is not just your artistic privilege you are exercising. Indeed, sometimes it seems the sole motivating force of your work. That frightens me.

I have now seen your illustrations for Baudelaire's *Les Fleurs du Mal.* Even though you complain that you did not have enough time to execute them and that many of the illustrations are adaptations of your old drawings of Dante's circles of hell or sketches after your figures for the colossal doors, I feel that I am looking at something brand new and altogether different. Perhaps that is why I admire your work so much and why, no matter how hard I struggle, I cannot stop loving you.

You always astound me. I can look at a figure of yours over and over again and each time find something so new and so alarming that I must ask myself if I really know you after all, or if I am just a lovesick young woman who cannot free herself from love's unfortunate spell.

What do you think that love or sex or torment is? That is the question I ask myself after viewing these illustrations. There is no simple answer. There are only layers of answers. It is not just the way the drawing itself informs the page.

It is the way the sketch adorns the poem, the way it hugs the margin, or the way the devil's toe curls down upon a phrase. For, after all, these are not simply drawings but illustrations, and you have placed them so that they have a dialogue not only with the poem they decorate but with the entire page. You have employed your genius so well at this that anyone who complains you have no architectonic sense is simply a fool.

But here again, this placing of the figure with its back up against the phrases gives me yet another answer to my questions, and my head spins with the possibilities of what you really think. I suppose it is a clever hoax to allow people to believe that because you are timid, you are simple. You are anything but simple. You are the most convoluted soul I have ever encountered. Perhaps that is why you intrigue me so much, and why I never tire of the excitement and new ideas your work brings me.

1 8 8 8

Rodin,

I admit that I was wrong when long ago I suggested you might benefit from sitting for a bust the way a composer benefits from listening to music. Clearly, you cannot. It is irritating to try to concentrate on sculpting your bust when you cannot sit still, but mainly I feel sorry for you. I will finish this bust, and it will be an acute and perspicacious interpretation of your head. But it seems that you will never allow yourself the experience of being a model. By your impatience and irritability you prevent yourself from feeling what it is like to be scrutinized, to be devoured by someone's gaze, to be sucked whole into someone else's vision. This kind of surrender and abandon is so delicious, so complete, it is almost a religious experience. I am sorry you will never feel it.

You see how my *Çacountala* is received in the Salon. I wish you wouldn't insist on always calling it *The Surrender*. That is not what it depicts. Your favorite moment in love might be the moment of surrender. That would suit your need always to dominate. My *Çacountala* depicts a moment of tenderness after lovemaking, when the young woman is spent and the young man is compelled by an irrepressible urge to express his tenderness for her. So you see how it is not what you think.

You rent La Folie Neuborg, the apartments of George Sand and Alfred de Musset, as if to say that two artists can love each other as equals. But then you will not admit knowing of their union or of their having rented the place, and you still will not leave Rose. I have agreed to live with you here because I am hoping that things will change between us, not because I agree to your conditions.

It's a pity, because the garden is so beautiful. Its wildness reminds me of the moor near Villeneuve, the Geyn, where as a child I used to take my brother Paul walking. On the moor I used to sit quietly and stare at the gigantic rocks as they changed shape before my eyes. Usually they would change from one strange monster shape to another, but sometimes they would take the shapes of jaguars or gazelles, or mimic the shapes of clouds. Paul was always frightened of them.

It is much the same here at the Folie. If I sit very quietly (I do this, of course, after you have gone home to a wife you do not love), the wild, untameable bushes begin to change shape, to twist and entwine, much like your figures for the doors, and as they writhe, their relationships to each other change—much the way you and I are always changing. Sometimes I envision you in the garden. Much time has passed. You are old. Your hair is completely white and your beard reaches down over your knees. You are kneeling, so the tip of your beard grazes the mossy garden floor. You are weeping. You finally realize that you should have chosen me, but it is too late now. Your love was wasted on others. Now you cannot get me out of your heart or your thoughts. So you've returned to the Folie, where other lovers lived a full life, to confess your own mistake, to try to leave the image of my face here. You want this garden to take back my soul, but even admitting your own folly will not be enough to achieve that. I will never leave you now, not ever. I will be with you always.

1 8 8 9

Rodin,

It is no wonder Mirbeau likes your *Embracing Women.* I hear his wife is also of that ilk. But he has praised you for so long that you should not lose your temper with him now. You know you look for glory in its most insipid forms, and you cannot reject your closest friends because they acknowledge it. Most people of your circle would think that allowing yourself to be made a chevalier of the Legion of Honor is wrong-headed. You can't make humoring your whims a condition of friendship, otherwise you will lose all your friends one by one in these petty squabbles. I say forgive Mirbeau and talk to him again. He has been your best supporter and critic. Don't reject him over a trifle.

1 8 8 9

Rodin,

I am glad we are giving ourselves another chance to be together, and that we are giving this house another chance. What an overgrown, untamed place it is! Like our love affair, it would need a good weeding and some new paint to even begin to look presentable, but of course we will let it go.

What a decadent old house. I am almost afraid of walking around in it sometimes for fear of disturbing its previous occupants. Surely they must have been rich and important, and by virtue of their position in Paris society would never have willingly relinquished ownership of the house, and even now may not have done so.

I do not know what to make of these new drawings you are doing here. Is this the way you drew the circles of hell after Dante? You draw so quickly, paying no heed to what you are doing, and you move on to the next sketch so fast, as if you were an insatiable madman. You act as though you realized you had lost me once and are trying to seize me now to prevent it from happening again. I have never witnessed such urgency, and I am not sure I understand what it is all about. But I am not criticizing you. On the contrary, I feel that something very important is happening that one day will be revealed to me. Right now I don't understand what it is.

Perhaps I might understand better if I imagined that you feel, making these sketches, the way that I do fashioning your bust. Sometimes, when I am working on it, I feel it has a greater power over me than I do over it. Perhaps that is why, when you work on your sketches, you sometimes seem overwhelmed, like a man possessed.

1 8 8 9

Monsieur Rodin,

You needn't worry that I am still working for you. You worked for others until you were forty, and I am still only twenty-five. What I think troubles you is that I can model your figures with so much ease, that everyone prefers me to mix their plaster, that I finish my marbles before anyone else, and that your graphite corrections are all superfluous.

I loved Cannes, not because I cherish your artist-friends (for Renoir, like the rest of them, is your friend, not mine), but because I love the sea so much.

Yes, the sea. I know it means nothing to you, you who pretend to love Nature so much. But you only love what you can conquer, and in Nature that would be only the twig, the leaf, the rock, the grass, and some women. Not myself.

I love the sea because its vastness comforts me. It clears my thoughts. It provides me with a limit but at the same time something in which I can lose myself.

What the cathedral does for you, the sea does for me. We are not so different, you and I, except that you allow only those things that you can dominate. You dominate the cathedral by studying it, you master it by solving its mysteries. I love the sea for precisely the opposite reason—it cannot be tamed. I respect the sea, I allow it to be itself.

But I do not understand why they all made such a commotion about those birds. Certainly, they could see how unhappy the poor things were, shut up like that, with hardly any air or light. I had to let them go. And to say that I am quaint and ingenuous to do so when it is they who live in the provinces! They live in Cannes. I live in Paris now, where one cannot afford to be ingenuous.

1 8 8 9

Rodin,

You were right to make me promises and to take me away to Tours just now. It is the only way you could win me back. I don't mean to sound proud or cruel. It's just that everything in Paris reminds me of all the pain I've suffered on your behalf, and there is no way to get relief from it, not even at our hideaway, La Folie Neuborg. Here, for a short time, there is nothing to distract us, one from the other, and I have the time to rediscover why I love you so much and why I want to be near you, even though it makes so much trouble in the end.

Even you seem to be rejuvenated by working here. You sleep better. Your stomach doesn't hound you. You concentrate better. You take solace in the countryside. I wish we could stay here indefinitely, living and working side by side, and did not have to return to Paris.

1 8 8 9

Rodin,

I'm sorry your new friends had to learn how selfish and domineering you can be. I know that Goncourt was astounded when he heard the news. Monet says he is devastated. And now you have lost another good friend because you insist on having your way and shoving his paintings into the background. Monet insists that both his work and yours could have been properly displayed, but you were ruthless and would only pick locations at his expense.

I suppose it should give me some comfort to see that you treat everyone shabbily and not just me, and that your other victims respond with the same sense of indignation that I have. But it does not make me feel any better. It only makes me wonder anew why you do it. It is so unnecessary. Both your sculptures and Monet's paintings could have been shown to advantage if you had been willing to go along with the placements you originally agreed upon.

I wish I knew how to make you understand, profoundly and finally, that no one is threatening you. You don't need to make others suffer to gain the advantage. Yet, I am at a loss to know how to accomplish this. Forgive me for not being a more resourceful partner. I am close enough to see how you harm yourself, but not ingenious enough to devise a preventive measure.

So will you make it up with Monet, or will you hold a grudge the way you usually do, coming to believe that it was you who were wronged by him? I wish we all didn't humor you and that you did not persist in casting out great men from your circle of friends every few months.

1 8 8 9

Rodin,

I am not surprised that amidst all the technical wonders of the Exposition—the Eiffel Tower, the electric lights, the multi-colored fountains—you find delight and perfection in that which is most remote from progress—the Javanese dancers. I would very much like to see the sketches you made of them.

1 8 9 0

Monsieur Rodin,

So what if I sat entranced and still in the face of Debussy's piano playing? I don't deny it. It is also true that he may be in love with me. We are companions, he and I, nothing more. He treats me with kindness and as an equal, the very things you are incapable of.

That is why you should be jealous of him, not because I am captured by his music, or because I have acquainted him with the Japanese art I love so much.

You should not be surprised that young men of genius are attracted to me and do not look upon me as your student. I am a great artist in my own right. I know how much you try to keep me associated with your older group of artists so I will be forever known as your student, but you cannot prevent my contemporaries from noticing me.

And you should stop tormenting yourself by wondering if that wonderful new piece by Debussy, "The Elusive Mademoiselle," was inspired by me. Of course it was.

Your whining about my not remaining loyal to you is utterly ridiculous. I already told you that I belong only to my art. But certainly, I would be loyal and faithful if you married me. It is you who cannot leave Rose.

You needn't be angry. It is true Debussy loves me, but I am not going to marry him. I wish I could, because he offers me the companionship of equals that I want so much from you.

But I cannot marry him because I do not love him. Don't gloat over this (I know you will); I don't fail to love him because I love you, but for some other reason I don't understand. Some say that I should marry him anyway, save my good name and my reputation, live among artists who are my peers instead of your decrepit friends, who are members of the Academy in their hearts, even when they refuse to join. As I said, I wish I could do it. But I know it would ruin me to marry a man I don't love, just as it might ruin me to love a man like you, who won't marry me.

Also, in addition to my not loving him, he has another woman whom he has lived with since he was very young. She is said to be beautiful and to have green eyes. Even her name, Gabrielle Dupont, is beautiful. Frankly, I am tired of the Other

Woman. I know he says he loves me, but you said you loved me (finally), and that did no good for us either.

No, I'm afraid I am tired. You needn't be so concerned.

The story has come back to me of how you've stolen Pierre Louÿ's model from him. I don't know what to think about this. She was his only mistress. He even came to your studio and pleaded for her return, but still you wouldn't surrender her. You can have any model in the Pigalle marketplace, yet you steal them away from other artists. I do not mean to scold you; I am just befuddled by it all. In a few weeks you will abandon this girl for some other you cannot live without.

1 8 9 1

Rodin,

I am glad that we can undertake the adventure of the *Balzac* monument together. It seems more like destiny than coincidence that our summer place in Tours is so close to the Château de Saché where Balzac wrote his *Lily of the Valley*, and we can combine some repose with a pilgrimage to seek out Balzac types.

I think you are right to search for them through his shape and not the reverse. I am sure that if we look diligently, we will find other men of his ilk who fit the image you have in your imagination. Remember, it is what you see in your heart that matters, that must take precedence.

1 8 9 1

Monsieur Rodin,

Must you persist in torturing yourself about Debussy? I told you that it was over between us, and that I shall not marry him. But you insist on pretending that you are tormented by his love for me. You needn't go with the others to his studio if my figure of the *Waltz* on his mantelpiece haunts you as much as you claim. I don't know why you visit his studio at all, when you're always complaining that you don't like Debussy's music. He does not like your figures either; he dismisses them as gamy romanticism.

I think you persist in this association just to goad me, just to remind me that he would have married me, though you never will, and then to twist it into your torment, your jealousy, to hide the true fact that it is you who have rejected me by not marrying me.

1 8 9 2

Rodin,

I'm sorry that my brother Paul is so ungrateful. After all, it was you who had him admitted to the foreign service examination by your letter to the foreign minister. Now that he's become a junior officer, it seems that he only insults us both—I am insufferable, and you are a lecherous boor—or at least that's what I hear through intermediaries. It seems that the hatred of art I saw in him when he was a child has only gathered fury as he's grown older, instead of being mediated by education, as I hoped it would be. But it seems quite the opposite—the more position and status he acquires in the government, the more he chooses to vent his spleen upon everything he dislikes, the main things being you, me, and the art world.

1 8 9 2

Monsieur Rodin,

You pretend you don't know that I am carrying your child. This does not astonish me. Then you let me come to the darling Islette early, before you have arrived, and stay on after you've gone, as if you knew I needed time to plan and arrange things, to enter into a conspiracy with Madame Courcelles concerning your child.

You assent mutely to these proceedings, as if you understood what must be done, and consented to this grave undertaking. But once again, sir, you are mistaken. I did not come here to put your child to rest, as you so blithely assume, as if the events of the world were fashioned after your preferences.

No, sir. I plan to give birth to this baby. I can see that you don't understand. Why, you ask. I will tell you why. (You see how doubly glad I am that I kept my vow never to give you these letters. Now, as always, I can speak freely.) I will have this baby simply because it is yours. I know I am too proud and do nothing but complain to you because you will not leave Rose and marry me (which you should do), but the truth is I do love you. I'm afraid that I will never love anyone again the way I have loved you. You see, I already speak of it in the past tense. If I cannot have you (and it is clear to me now I cannot), then I can have your child. In this way, I will never really lose you in body the way I have lost the sight of you. This way, I will be able to enter your child's soul, the way I have never been able to enter yours. I tried to win it, to lure it, to steal it. I tried to be frank and straightforward. But you will not let me inside, not for anything.

I am not fooling myself. I know the child will be a torment to me. I will have to hide him from Paris and from my family. But I will love him frankly and truly, the way I love you, the way my father loves me.

1 8 9 2

Rodin,

I am not surprised to be cradling your son in my arms—for some reason I cannot explain, I knew I was carrying a son and not a daughter—but I would not have expected to be holding *two* sons. I should have known; I had grown much too large to have been carrying only one of your children. I have named them both after you. The son who was born a minute earlier is named François, and the one who was born a minute later is named René. So now with your son Auguste by Rose (whom you do not love as you love me, and should not have chosen over me), you now have three sons, each bearing one of your three Christian names.

I have given them the family name of Athanaïse. It was my mother's middle name and my maternal grandfather's first name. It's a beautiful name, isn't it? François Athanaïse. René Athanaïse. I chose the name because I did not want your sons tormented by having to carry your name or mine, and my mother's maiden name, Cerveaux, is too easily linked to me. Your sons will be safe and prosper under this name. My grandfather, who bore this name, was a doctor.

I am sorry you will never know that your two sons exist or get to see them face to face and know they are your sons. (I'm sure, when they are old enough, they will want to sneak out to Paris to take a look at you.) I am sorry I had to seem to go along with your belief that I came to Azay-le-Rideau to get rid of my children, and that I have stayed on so long because I could not recover from their loss, when really it has taken all this time to bring them into the world.

I want to assure you that although I will not give up my art or my good name in order to raise your sons, they will be in good hands here with Madame Courcelles. I will see them as often as I can. They will know from the very beginning that I am their mother, and they will know as soon as they are old enough that you are their father. I will never slander you to them. You can believe that. The criticisms I level at you in these letters and in person are between us. They will know your good qualities, and I will answer their questions about your limitations as diplomatically as I can.

I have known all along that both my life and work were leading toward some great secret. Now it is suddenly revealed to me in its many facets. I keep the secret from you that you have two sons by me. I keep the same secret from my family, from Paris, from the world. I keep the secret from you that I am breaking off our relations because of your sons. I keep the secret from myself that somehow, amidst all of this, my heart has died, and it cannot be reawakened.

I am sorry you think my bust of you is all wrong, that the brow is too noble, the eyes too sad, the nose too virile, the mouth too sensual, the beard too forceful, and the overall effect too beautiful. I think it is perfect. I did not expect you to like it or even approve, just as I did not like your *Thought*, in which you used my face.

Just as you, in your *Thought*, portrayed my face to evoke the emotions that you feel for me, so I have similarly done in my bust of you. The sadness around the eyes and cheeks, the longing in the forehead—that is what I feel when I look at you now. As far as beauty is concerned, you are beautiful. I don't deny that, no matter how angry I might be for the way you treat me. The tenderness in the face is, of course, not your tenderness but the tenderness I feel for you.

I should not need to explain these things to you, you who pretend to understand everything about art.

1 8 9 3

Rodin,

It is probably best that you move to Bellevue with Rose. She will be happier in the suburbs, and you will enjoy the boat ride to Paris. You will have the city and its diversions separate from Rose, and perhaps the distance will spare her some of the humiliation and jealousy she must feel. You see what a reasonable person I can be when I do not feel hurt and angry. She must be as unhappy as I am, and there is no reason to malign her with insults.

I hope you will think of me when you go on long walks in the forest there and become so troubled that your dog will wonder at it and press his wet nose into the palm of your hand.

Thank you for your kind letter about my two figures at the Salon. But I would, of course, prefer that you did not write to me, as I have already stated, even if it is to praise me. I see through your praise. That is not to say that your praise is not sincere; I believe it is. But to praise me for figures such as

Clotho is to praise me for working in your style, for following in your footsteps, for remaining forever your student. I do not plan to do that. Now that I am rid of you (and I am, you know), I will pursue my own vision, and everyone will see that it owes nothing to yours, except for you and your colleagues, who will remain forever ignorant of my genius.

I would never really tell you of these sculptures, because you would at once set about to undermine them. But since you will never read these letters, I may speak freely.

As I told you before in these letters, the real work I have been hiding from you consists of tiny figures, miniatures of sculpture. My favorite is the *Gossipers*, several women listening to another, garnering her secrets. You see how the topic of secrets always arises. The figures are enclosed by a screen. I envision this piece in onyx, but of course I have no money for such extravagances.

There will be another group, very similar, of three young girls holding hands under an enormous wave that has risen up and is about to envelop them.

I am sure you will steal this idea from me after it is exhibited, since you like so much the idea of possession, especially Nature possessing young girls. But the air of mystery in these tiny sculptures will escape you when you try to copy them, even if you try to make the wave into the image of God's hand, as I know you will. I know you too well.

Many other miniatures like these will follow: a girl kneeling against a hearth, a girl gazing into the fireplace (it is usually cold here, as you must know, and living in my studio, I must keep the fire going constantly). There will be a scene at the dinner table, farmers in a wagon, children listening in astonishment to a violin player, and many others I have already planned, if I can survive forever on no money. Already, my creditors are hounding me, my mother and sister despise me, my brother barely helps me. Of course, you won't help. You watch in secret glee while I sink deeper and deeper into indebtedness and shame, hoping I won't realize my genius, all the while writing me false letters of praise to disguise the fact that you want me to fail.

It seems only natural, now that your sons are born, that I should return to Paris and, instead of continuing to live with my family, move into my studio on the Boulevard d'Italie. Since you have already abandoned our Folie Neuborg and moved with Rose to Bellevue, I needn't worry about seeing you nearby at the Folie nor fear that I have misunderstood your decision.

You should not be surprised by this. It was you who fled the Folie Neuborg while I was in Tours, so full with your sons. It was you who moved with Rose to Bellevue instead of installing her there alone while you stayed in Paris.

It is beginning to enrage me less that you remain with Rose when you really love me and could only be happy with me, because I am beginning to understand your complacency, your fear of equality and true feeling. But I am becoming more and more infuriated by your inability to take responsibility for your own choices. Why do you blame me for not submitting to your whims? It is you who choose Rose over me again and again, you who choose to live with her and legitimize her. It is you who refuse to marry me. Failure to act is a choice. Abdication is a choice. You might as well admit it. But then, if you did, you would be admitting a shortcoming, a failure in your life, and you are not capable of that, are you, just as you are not capable of treating any woman well.

Tonight I am sitting in my studio, staring at *The Waltz*, waiting for it to be packed up and taken to the Société Nationale des Beaux-Arts to be exhibited for the first time.

I wonder why you don't like this sculpture. Is it because it does not resemble yours? Is it because the young woman is embracing a young man her own age and not someone older? Is it because the young man lets her be herself and does not try to dominate her? Is it because the young man is physically beautiful, well-built, graceful, and tender? Is it because the young man is so attentive in the way he's leaning toward the young woman, as if he were listening to her very being? Or is it simply because the couple slants precariously to one side and creates an aura of tension that you could not discover and display in your own work?

You are a stubborn man.

1894

Rodin,

I wish we were still seeing each other so that I might console you about your *Balzac*. You have made an extensive pilgrimage into Balzac's life. You have walked through the countryside where he lived, searching for types, you have read his biographies, looked through photos, even had a suit made by his tailor. You have made sketch after sketch and become disenchanted with each one in turn.

Now you believe you are lost, that all this searching has led you further and further from the man, and that in becoming so steeped in his milieu, you have lost his essence.

That is, of course, the danger, but that is not what has happened. As always, you are simply impatient. You have perhaps become lost in details for the moment, and for the moment lost sight of the true man, but that is only part of the journey you are taking to find him. And you will find him. Be patient. Have faith in your abilities to find what you are looking for, to know when you have found it, and to persist until you do find it. It is no small accomplishment to create a monument to a man who is greater than yourself, and also to make it a true work of genius. This is the task you set yourself. Of course, it is going to take several years and a dozen maquettes before you find what you are looking for.

Why do we think it should be easy? Why do we think we should know the answer the minute we have gathered the information? Why do we think we shouldn't have to suffer, that this work should be full of success and glory and ease of execution?

In this muddle of information you have gathered you will

rediscover the man you are looking for. Trust yourself to do it, and do not settle for less. Your heart will tell you when you have found him.

I am having quite a pleasant time here in Guernsey with Monsieur Hugo's grandson Georges. My only ill feeling is that if I am away from Paris, I should be with your sons. But Madame Courcelles convinced me that I was under too much strain, having broken with you just before your sons were born, and that I needed a complete diversion. She said everyone does at least once in their life, and I should not be ashamed of it.

I do not understand why you should be so upset at my coming here that you would tell Roger Marx you no longer have any authority over me. Perhaps you think the Hugos your sole province just because of the bust you made of Victor ten years ago. But my acquaintance with Georges comes through my brother Paul, not through you, so you shouldn't believe you have the right of control over it.

1 8 9 4

Monsieur Rodin,

There. I have done it. I have suffered your sons to sit for a composite bust so you can at least see their likeness, though you still will not know they are yours. I have made the bust into a girl by giving it a braid of hair to further prevent you from knowing. The bust is called *La Petite Châtelaine* and is quite good. Both François and René were delighted with it, since they look the same. It is René's sense of wonderment that I have captured in the expression. Being the younger, he seems to have the greater capacity for awe. They are only two now, and though I don't see them nearly enough, I see them as often as I am able, and Madame Courcelles is very kind.

It occurs to me, now that your sons are two, that I never explained in my letter why you will never know of your new sons. It is so simple that perhaps it did not occur to me to mention it. It is simply this: you do not want to marry me. After ten years, that had become abundantly clear. Now, what if I had told you about your sons and you had offered to marry me? The indignity of it would have been too much to bear. I have my pride. So now you understand the reason.

You might also be wondering why I always refer to them as your sons instead of as ours. There are two reasons. We share nothing now, since you have stolen my heart, my soul, my works of art, my particular figures, my lines, my poses, even my face. Since nothing is ours, it must be either mine or yours.

Why are they not mine, then? I don't know. I love them. I carried them. I see them as often as I can. But there is a way in which they are lost to me that I felt the moment they were conceived and continue to feel to this day. I don't understand it exactly or I would explain it to you. Maybe someday I will understand better.

1 8 9 5

Rodin,

I am worried about your health. If I were still seeing you, I would try to coax you away from all these banquets. I am sure that you are eating too much. It is no wonder you are suffering from insomnia when in one sitting you can eat crayfish bisque, salmon, trout, leg of venison, fattened pullet with truffles, pheasant and partridge, lobster, artichoke hearts and asparagus tips, and you can drink a glass of Madeira, one of Pommard, another of Fronsac, and another of iced champagne. No, of course you are depressed. The confusion to the palate alone must be overwhelming.

I have already written you what I thought of your *Balzac*, as you requested through the intermediary Monsieur Le Bossieu, so I don't think it fair of you to complain that I haven't given you all my thoughts on the matter. And of course this complaint reaches me as you intended it to. Why can't you accept the respectful praise I have already given you? Why is it never enough? Why, in addition to having loved and wanted you, do you insist that I admire you? I don't think it is kind or polite to request that a woman reveal all her thoughts on a subject. Since when has that ever been required?

But if you must know the rest (and, of course, with your cunning, you sensed it), I will tell it to you here, since you will never read these pages.

I knew when I saw your *Balzac* that this was the true expression of your genius—your evil genius, perhaps. The colossal doors and your tormented figures for them may be the perfect expression of your *oeuvre*, but this *Balzac*, which pretends to represent the prolific writer, is really an expression of your soul. It is a divine mirror reflecting back your own face. It told me two great secrets, one that I knew and another that I didn't. It told me you do indeed see yourself for the sacred monster you are, and do perhaps suffer for it. It also told me that we are finished, you and I. It made me certain of it.

I warned you that my *Gossipers* would be a work of genius that even you could not fail to recognize. Now that you have seen it at the Salon du Champs de Mars, don't you agree that it is exquisite? I know you don't understand or appreciate the precious, you who are concerned only with that which is prolific or gargantuan. But here is the precious raised to the level of art, and I am pleased that you have finally seen it at the Salon, even though you may find some way to claim authorship of it. Now I'm sure you can understand why I refused to let you into my studio to see the new work. You would have wanted desperately to steal it, and with all your money, supplies, and apprentices (of which you offer me none), you could easily have reproduced it and exhibited it before I had had the chance. At least now I have proven once and for all that this work is mine, and you will have to become ever more cunning to invent new ways to rob me. I'm sure you will succeed in the end, but in the meantime I take great pleasure in watching you realize, gazing at my new work, that I can quite easily create art that has nothing to do with you or the love we had for each other, just as you created your *Balzac.* I had to prove it to you. I have never felt more triumphant than at this moment.

1895

Rodin,

My brother Paul has returned from his consular position in America. He had the courtesy to invite me to dinner with his friend Jules Renard, but I'm afraid he no longer even pretends to tolerate me. Before I even speak, his entire expression changes, and throughout the entire meal he looks as though he were trying to hold back a torrent of abuse.

I have received your request via Mirbeau that you be invited to his house the same day I am. Mirbeau, of course, can do whatever he chooses; it is his house. But I told him that if you were invited that day, I would come another time.

I don't mean to be harsh or to reject you repeatedly. I know you are suffering as much as I am because of our separation, and my heart goes out to you. But please understand that I absolutely cannot see you again. I have explained all the reasons so many times before, I will not repeat them here. Please do not try, through whichever intermediaries, to arrange a meeting between us.

I will admit to you here, in this moment of sympathy between us, that life is indeed sad for me. I am able to continue to work, and I enjoy the work and my solitude. I spend whole afternoons copying in the Louvre or taking walks around unfamiliar parts of the city. The people I see there give me ideas for new groupings and, thus inspired, I go back to my studio and work. But I must confess that I have little heart for seeing my old friends. The Daudets are kind enough to invite me, and the Schwobs and the Pottechers often ask me to dinner. But even when I try to go, I end up standing outside in the hedges, staring in the windows instead of going inside.

It is not simply that I have nothing to wear. Sometimes this is a real hindrance or an embarrassment, and if I do not earn some money soon, it will become a real problem. But that is what I seize on when I am angry because it is simple and clear. Something much deeper is wrong. It is as though my heart had died. I can't believe this is true, since I am still able to work. But I can no longer be around people. My whole body rejects it. I become sullen and withdrawn, if I am able to go out at all. The only people I can stand to be around now are your sons. They are so delightful. They are the only thing besides work that brings me joy. I'm afraid that I am overcome with sadness at no longer being near you. That must be it. Being with others must remind me of not being with you and therefore aggravate the wound. At least here alone in my studio, working, I can find some peace.

1 8 9 5

Rodin,

I am worried about your reaction to Bing's opening exhibition at his Galerie de l'Art Nouveau. Perhaps you were overcome by an impulse to support your friend Goncourt. But to say that an international style is barbaric! To defend the maintenance of a French style at all costs!

I know you are a conservative when it comes to politics and life (except in your dealings with women, in which you make an exception for selfish reasons). But I never thought you would become conservative in your thinking about art. Your whole life you have dedicated yourself to making innovations in art, you have shocked the public and critics with your innovations. Do you now forbid others to make these same innovations? Or do you make progress in art in spite of yourself?

You have not stopped searching for a new truth in art. Your struggles with the *Calais* and *Balzac* monuments are proof of that, as are your quick sketches of the female form. So I do not understand why you can no longer allow that search to others. Don't you see that your criticism of an international artistic style is just as narrow-minded as the critics' reaction to your own work?

I know that eventually you will become part of the older generation of artists, and young artists will feel the need to reject your style, as I have, and find their own. But I did not think that your vision would be narrowed and that you would no longer be able to appreciate progress and innovation in art.

After all, internationalism is where art in Paris is headed. Everyone comes here from other countries now. In the next ten or twenty years, the new art that is formed will have to be, by its very nature, international. That is the future. I can't believe that you don't understand and welcome this as the next innovation. Should innovation stop with your own work? Is your truth the only truth?

I suppose what I am really afraid of is that this new conservatism of yours signals an end to innovation in your own work. I hope this is not true.

1 8 9 6

Rodin,

I hear you have actually bought the Villa des Brillants in Meudon. Frankly, I was surprised by the news. I did not realize you had so much money. It sounds like it must be a very spacious house if you have room in the outbuildings to make coops for Rose's canaries. The view of Sèvres, St-Cloud and the Seine as far as the Trocadéro sounds exquisite. And you already have a studio with skylights. What could be more convenient? And with such an expansive house, you will have all the room you need to display the art you've been collecting, your friends' paintings on the second floor, your Oriental bronzes and Egyptian statuettes in the bedroom, your own pieces in the studio.

Rose will continue to be completely away from Paris and your escapades, and you will continue to be able to get away from Paris when the strain becomes too great, but now to your very own house.

Since I know your fear of fires, I worry about how you will be able to heat and light such a big house. Does it have gas or electricity? Those vegetable oil lamps are so inconvenient.

I also hear that now that you have moved into the house, you do not seem so tired, and you are beginning to work again.

I am glad of it. I envy you finding a place of your own where you can be comfortable and at peace. Only then can we find the concentration we need to sustain our work. I envy what you have made for yourself. I wish I could share it with you, especially the peace.

1896

Monsieur Rodin,

Don't be absurd in your accusations. You are growing paranoid in your old age. I have moved from the Boulevard d'Italie because I needed a change of air. I am not trying to "hide" from you as you claim, though I have asked you not to send me messages and invitations, and I do wish you would stop so I needn't insist on it so emphatically.

To be honest (since you won't be reading these), I left the Boulevard d'Italie because it was making me melancholy. It was too near the Folie Neuborg and our good times together, when you began, for a moment, to treat me kindly, and I still hoped that you might realize I was your salvation and that you should stay with me.

Now you are lost, and I am alone and a bit sad. So I moved to brighter quarters, where perhaps I can forget about what might have been possible, put out of my mind the euphoria that would have been our life together working side by side.

The Boulevard d'Italie reminded me of those possibilities. It is best now to rid myself of all possibilities that remind me of you. That is why I began my new work, my true work of secrets in miniature; they give me so much pleasure.

Perhaps I can find peace here with my new work and will no longer have any reason to run away.

Since you will not listen to my polite requests, I have directed Monsieur Morhardt to tell you quite plainly not to visit me any more.

Why don't you believe me? Have I ever been coy? You must understand now what I have been trying to explain to you since your sons were born and your *Balzac* was conceived: it is over between us. It is cruel to force me to employ intermediaries. And even if it did not pain me to see you and prevent me from making progress with my new work which I love so much, I am now so broke trying to pay off creditors that I have no decent clothes in which to receive you or dine with you.

1897

Rodin,

You needn't be chagrined by these new rejections of your work. I know they come from all sides—the old and the young, the conservative and the modern. I could chide you and say you should be accustomed to it by now, but I know you expected that at least other artists would understand your work. I am afraid, dear man, that you are trapped in a world of your own and that you will continue to be attacked from all sides. I know that everything I am about to say is fatuous, but I will say it anyway in an effort to console you.

Ignore the Swedes. They are embroiled in politics of their own, and their rejection of the *Interior Voice* has no bearing on its merits. The Symbolists are blind and ignorant when they say that your work isn't human. They should be able to appreciate your art; but they are brash, and their need to reject older forms renders them unable to see what is novel in your work.

The reactions to your *Victor Hugo* monument at the Salon must be accepted in the same light as all your previous scandals there. Just as they did not understand the modeling of your *Age of Bronze* twenty years ago, they are outraged by the unfinished qualities of the monument. Instead of realizing that that is the direction in which your art is headed and hailing it as a stroke of genius, they criticize it as a craftsman's flaw, as if you didn't know what you were doing.

I know how dispiriting this barrage of criticism must be, especially now when you were just beginning to feel rested again and when you thought your reputation might make you immune to it. But I am afraid the truth is that your work will always outrage everyone, and that you will remain trapped inside the world of your own art, looking out at all the scandalized and famous people—young and old, artists, critics, and public—and you will feel completely alone.

This is the cross you must bear. Carry it with dignity and humility. Work in spite of it. Understand that this is simply the way the world works and that there is nothing personal in it.

1 8 9 8

Rodin,

I think that you have done the right thing for the wrong reason. Let me explain. I think it was right to keep the *Balzac* monument once it had been rejected by the committee, rather than sell it to the group of artists who had raised money by subscription to buy it. But it was wrong to do it for the reason you chose: that the group of artists who wished to buy it was pro-Dreyfusard. You should have chosen to keep it for artistic reasons, not in order to avoid being embroiled in a political squabble. I understand you are not political by nature (neither am I), and so you don't wish to involve yourself in political issues. But decisions about your art should be made for artistic reasons only, not for any reasons peripheral to art. I am anti-Dreyfusard as you are, and may lose my friendship with Monsieur Morhardt because of it, so I sympathize with your position at the same time as I voice my opinion.

Since I am sure now that our relationship is completely finished and that you will not bother me again by trying to speak or write to me, or by asking me to accompany you to your artistic functions, it is time we addressed this question of you stealing my works. I should not have to remind you, sir, that you worked as a decorative artist for Carrier-Belleuse and as an artisan with Van Rasbourg. You were more than a bit upset when these men claimed your vases, your caryatids, your colossal figures as their own. So you should not be surprised to learn that I am outraged to hear you plan to exhibit my works as yours. It is easy for you, the great Parisian master, as they call you, to go to the Universal Exposition and accept the praise and acclaim for my sculptures. Who would believe me, a struggling sculptress, over you, the great master? I would not be surprised if I went down in history as your student and, as a result, my *Çacountala* is then believed to have been modeled on your *Eternal Springtime*, my *Young Woman with a Sheaf* copied from your *Galatea*, my *Old Helen* a study of your *She Was Once the Helmet Maker's Beautiful Wife*, my *Torso of a Crouching Woman* borrowed from yours, my *Man Leaning* a variation of your *Thinker*, my *Waltz* done in homage to your *Kiss*.

But we both know, don't we, that you have stolen all these works from me, that mine was the initial conception, the original pose, the innovative line, and that it was you who copied (in the name of your colossal doors) and believed it just, because you were the so-called master and I the student.

But do not be misled. I am putting my lawyers to the great chore of unmasking you, and they will work long and hard at the task. I am not naïve; I know that the truth may not be revealed in your lifetime or mine, but someday it will be uncovered. Someday the world will know that not only did you steal my heart, my will, my position in society, my reputation, and my potential as a great artist, but you stole my very work, one by one you expropriated my figures. And everyone will be made to realize that you did not do this unknowingly or unwittingly or even nobly for the sake of art; you did it ruthlessly and deliberately to subjugate me.

Someday they will all know it. They will see who you are. For now, I am forced to suffer the torment of reading the praise heaped on you for my sculptures. I am asked to watch silently while you receive all the adulation and glory for my work. And then you reproach me for being bitter.

And the plot does not end with theft. You must thwart my commissions as well. First, you blocked the commission your colleague Puvis de Chavannes tried to secure for me, to install my *Clotho* in the Luxembourg Museum in his honor. I know very well why that project died. Now you are attempting to thwart Monsieur Morhardt's efforts to secure for me the commission for the Alphonse Daudet monument.

Why do you do it? You know I cannot pay for clay and marble and armatures with the meager sums I receive to fashion lamps and ashtrays. You know I will never be able to support myself making busts if I am not legitimized in the public eye by a commission.

But you neglect to speak to Leon Daudet and Monsieur Mirbeau, as Morhardt asked you to, because you know your neglect will quickly ruin the project and they will ask someone else. Then you pretend to have forgotten. And since you have pretended for so long to be my mentor, Morhardt believes you. He doesn't see through your plan to destroy me. But I do. And I warn you. You will not manage it. I will survive—on pure bitterness, if that's all that is left to me—and I will have my day. It is you who will be ruined, ultimately. It is you, the great master, who will be shown as a liar and a thief, thwarting an innocent young woman's career and then pirating her creations. Raphael was avenged for the thefts of Perugino, Van Dyck for the thefts of Rubens. I too will be avenged.

I just want to point out to you that although you persecute me, and sometimes succeed in blocking commissions that would otherwise be awarded to me (witness the Puvis de Chavannes tribute and *Daudet* monument), I still prevail.

With the kind patronage of Maurice Fenaille, who is not easily tricked and does not believe your lies, I have been able to complete the *Wave*. And what a beauty it is! I have even been able to have a copy made in onyx as I dreamed of.

Of course, you will steal it the minute you see it exhibited, and turn the great *Wave* into your hand or some such vain, silly nonsense, but I will know the beauty of it is mine, and Monsieur Fenaille will know. Even though I have exhibited in three Salons for fifteen years, though I show at two galleries, though the critics praise my work and proclaim me the greatest French sculptor, I still cannot secure the commission that would give me the financial security to proceed with my work, that would legitimize me in the eyes of my family and the public, and that would provide me with a wardrobe that would allow me to leave my studio without being ridiculed by urchins and whispered about by neighbors. My family and the public still believe you, and my commissions are blocked.

You needn't grieve so much about losing me. I know how unhappy you are. Of course, the news gets back to me—for example, the display you put on at Monsieur Morand's lunch the other day, in which you frightened his children.

I wish you would admit that it was your decision instead of making everyone believe that I abandoned you. You were the one who would not live with me, who would not leave Rose, who would not marry me. It was your choice, not mine.

Yes, I have moved to the Quai Bourbon, and what of it? I needed to be farther away from you, closer to the Seine, surrounded by water. And furthermore, my landlord evicted me for not paying the rent.

1899

Rodin,

I am in despair. I don't know how to make you understand that all your little attempts to help me make me more and more unhappy, and that I must be completely alone and completely free of you if I am ever to recover from losing you.

I have tried in many different ways to tell you this. I have explained it to you logically and sensibly. I have lost my temper and railed at you. I have begged and pleaded with you. In short, I have tried everything. Still, you send me these Scottish sculptresses, asking for lessons and saying that I have been recommended by you.

I know that you mean well, that you are not trying to hurt me. But why don't you believe what I have told you so many times? I don't want to see you. I don't want to receive messages from you through intermediaries. I don't want you to try to obtain commissions for me. I don't want to exhibit with you. I don't want you to arrange for articles to be written about me. I don't want you to send me students. I don't want to have any contact with you at all.

I suppose you cannot put yourself in my place. But try anyway. Imagine you are me. You are trying to get over a man who for fifteen years has dominated you and your work and treated you badly. You find that your only solace is to be alone and to work at your art. Any thought of that man reminds you not only of your present hurt, but of the past fifteen years of humiliation and unhappiness at his hands.

And yet this man will not leave you alone. Every day he does something to make you think of him. You ask him in every way imaginable to stop, but he does not. Now he sends you young sculptresses of the age you were when you fell in love with him, so you will be reminded of that. Surely you can understand. What must I do to make you stop?

So your painter friend Fritz Thaulow has told Henrik Ibsen "everything" about us, and Ibsen in turn has written a play on the subject that has just been published. I am curious: Did Thaulow tell Ibsen what he observed, or have you been making confessions? Has the play been read to you? And when it is translated, will you read it? When the play is staged in Paris, will you attend the opening?

I am almost tempted to go with you, if you do go, more as an act of defiance than a gesture of approval. Of course, I do not approve. My sculptures should be exhibited, but my personal life should not be interpreted (by an infamous misogynist, no less) and displayed to the world. It's an outrage.

Yes, it's true that we do busts and monuments of dead artists without their consent, and that the results are often revealing and outrageous to the public. Your *Balzac* (your only true work of genius, which could not have been conceived if I had not inspired you to undergo the preparatory exercise of your colossal doors) is the prime example. It is too revealing for many; no wonder they are outraged. And the busts we do of living artists, even commissioned, are never really approved of or sanctioned. Again, because they are too revealing.

But I protest these criticisms of our work. Our busts and monuments are not interpretations, they are not attempts to convey information. They are works of art and stand alone without reference, regardless of how they were inspired.

So why doesn't Ibsen's play deserve the same immunity? I am not sure. Perhaps I suspect him of bad intentions, of setting about to spread gossip and innuendo instead of to create art. Since he is already known as a great artist, this charge has no basis. Perhaps, then, I am wrong and simply resent the sacrifice of my personal life to the service of art. Haven't I already made that sacrifice once? I suppose I shall have to read the play and decide for myself if it transcends the merely anecdotal. But I am self-taught in literature, as you are, and since I am also sensitive to being the play's subject, I am not sure that I could objectively judge.

1900

Rodin,

I do not know what to think of your new liaisons with young women of position. I am not jealous, because there is no longer any risk for you in it, and so I know they cannot really touch your soul as I did.

I wonder what it is like for you now to conquer a young woman. You have such a reputation. Do they expect it and feel snubbed if you do not approach them, and so you feel obliged? Has it become a form of introduction, like exchanging names? Do you still feel the same thrill of possession you once did in the lean years when you were alone with Rose and had not yet fully exercised your artist's prerogative? Or is it less urgent, less frantic, more of the subtle pleasure that a pipe smoker or a connoisseur of rare cognac might feel?

I wish I knew if anyone, at this moment, truly touches your

heart. Is it the artistocrat Sophie von Hindenburg or her daughter Helen? Is it the American dancer Isadora Duncan? The painter Jelka Rosen who reads you Nietzsche? The Scottish sculptress Kathleen Bruce? I wish it could be me.

1902

Rodin,

I wish you would stop celebrating your success at the Universal Exposition and get back to work. I don't mean to scold you; I am simply worried that you will never work again, now that you are content and so busy socializing. That would be a great loss for art.

You are never in your studio anymore. It seems that all you do now is travel. I don't know how you tolerate it. First, you are off to Grez to visit Jelka Rosen. Then, you visit the Thaulows in Quimperlé. Next, you're off to Italy to visit the von Hindenburgs at the Villa Margherita in Ardenza and allow them to take you sightseeing in Serravezza, Lucca, and Pisa. Then, you're off to London to be honored by the Victoria and Albert Museum and the students at the Royal College of Art. Next, to Prague to preside over your exhibition there. Then, to Vienna to make an appearance at the Secession exhibit.

Where will it end? And when you are in Paris, you spend your time attending banquets in your honor, humoring young artists who are enthralled by you, lunching with the aristocrats and socialites who buy copies of your figures from the colossal doors and commission their own busts. In the meantime, you are being passed over for national commissions to do monuments because all your previous monuments remain unfinished or have been rejected by their sponsoring committees, and you have not produced one figure of importance since your *Balzac* five years ago.

I know that your apprenticeship was long. While many of the artists today are known in their twenties, you were not known until your forties, and now you are past sixty. But a late success is no reason to stop working in order to relish it.

Nothing is more important than continuing to create art. I thought you had more conviction. I did not know you could give up your work so easily.

1 9 0 2

Monsieur Rodin,

It is absurd to persist in this thinking that I am ruining my chances for success by refusing to exhibit with you. You must realize that if I continue to show my works next to yours, in Prague or whichever city invites it, I perpetuate the notion, in the minds of art critics and the public, that I am your student. I refuse to go down in history as your student, sir, and if this means waiting until I can show my work alone and be recognized for the artist I am, I will wait.

I object to this myth you insist on perpetuating, that you want to exhibit my sculptures with yours to make me famous, that you are giving me opportunities. As always, you are trying to subjugate me by making me known only in your shadow, all the while pretending that you are trying to help me.

I suppose it would be too much to ask that you be frank about your aims. That would spoil your plans to ruin me. The whole enterprise disgusts me. I will ask my lawyers to find a way to make you stop, even though I am penniless and can only pay them with copies of my work.

1 9 0 5

Rodin,

Once again I find myself apologizing to you for my brother. I'm afraid that as more time goes by and he rises in the ranks of the Ministry, he becomes more and more incensed against art, especially modern art. He seems to have made you the target of his abuse and vilification and wants to make an example of me.

I'm afraid I have no way of preventing him from publishing these articles about us in *L'Occident.* If it makes you feel any better, he attacks the Fauves in his latest article. I told you long ago (twenty-four years!) that he had an aversion to art. Since he was only a child when we moved to Paris for my sculpture and then I fell in love with you and became your student, I'm afraid that he connects my current situation as a neglected artist with you, even though you and I haven't seen each other in thirteen years.

You must try to forgive him for his shortsightedness. He has never felt any passion or known any love, nor does he understand the need to make sacrifices for art. As a result, all that is left to him is to try to fit us into his narrow scheme of things. That is his only hope of understanding us.

I know it is hard for you to forgive him. For me it is easy. It hurts me that he reviles you and tries to make an example of me, but he is my brother and I love him. I suppose, too, that since he has always been this way, I am accustomed to his bourgeois opinions.

In any case, put your mind at rest—he has taken a post in China and is leaving soon. Perhaps he will change his notions there or simply forget about us.

I have just finished carving my *Çacountala* into marble, and I am wondering what you will think of it. First, you will be jealous because I am such a good carver and do not need to consign the work to others as you do. Second, I think you would agree that whereas your figures look best in bronze, mine look best in marble. Next, you will be pleased that you have already exhibited *Eternal Springtime* and *Fugit Amor*, so people will believe my piece is inspired by yours, not the reverse. By studying the piece closely, you will realize that mine is the better sculpture. It is modulated perfectly. It is not marred by sentimentality like *Eternal Springtime* or by excessive zeal like *Fugit Amor*. It is true. And you will realize, though you will not admit it, that this perfection is not created by the surfaces or the modeling but by the lines. The lines in your *Eternal Springtime* are too rigid, those in *Fugit Amor* too arabesque. Mine are somewhere between, in that area you cannot find because it is too subtle, too precise. You haven't the patience to find it or the tenderness to recognize it if you did.

The rumors you hear about me are only partially true. It is true, for example, that in the summer I lock up my apartment and leave for several months without telling anyone where I am going. If you could read these letters, you would be able to surmise, of course, that I am going to the Islette to spend some time with your sons. Obviously, I cannot tell anyone where I am going. And even if I could, who would really want to know? My mother and sister despise me and are just looking for a way to get rid of me. My brother Paul is going to China, and even if he remained, his attempts to help me are, like yours, camouflages to conceal the fact that he is really trying to destroy me. My father, bless his poor heart, might want to know where I have gone, but my mother and sister hound him so for loving me that I could not bear to tell him.

As far as smashing my sculptures to pieces is concerned, that is also true. Since you will never read these letters, I can tell you that they are not the originals I destroy. I let the gossipmongers believe that to keep them off the track. No, I keep the original plaster cast in one safe location (which I will not reveal even here) and a bronze copy of each figure in another. It is true that this deception of mine is extremely costly, not only in time and money but in the damage it does to my good name. But I feel forced into it to preserve my art in the face of my mother's and sister's vengeance and my brother's and your thirst for revenge.

I am sorry to have to tell you that I am not the desperate lunatic you hoped I had become, just a destitute artist, struggling not only against poverty and the public's indifference but against the vicious intentions of my family and yourself to destroy me.

Your sons, if you must know, are big, strapping fellows at the great age of thirteen. They have, by some gift of Providence, escaped your childhood faults of weakness, shyness, and frailty and show no signs of assuming your adult faults of vanity, egotism, or an oppressive attitude toward women.

They also seem to have escaped my sin of hubris. You should consider yourself lucky to have two sons who are free both of your faults and their mother's.

Today I wrote my dealer, Eugène Blot, and turned down his invitation to accompany him to the Salon d'Automne because I am so poor that I have nothing to wear. My family and colleagues complain about how much I stay locked up in my studio, but when I beg for money to pay the rent or buy some clothes, no one helps me. Yesterday I was forced to borrow money from an acquaintance to pay the fines levied against me for not paying my creditors, and this acquaintance accused me of keeping a lover. I cannot tell you what indignities I suffer.

And, of course, you do nothing to help me, you who have grown rich and fat from the Universal Exposition. You could easily help me now, if you really wanted to save me from disgrace and embarrassment. But, of course, you don't want to see me succeed as an artist, because then you would be revealed as a fraud and a thief. No, you want me to fail, to rot away in obscurity in order to conceal your lies and foul doings and to preserve your false good name. I despise you.

1 9 0 6

Rodin,

I never thought I would be ashamed to have known you, but the rumors I've been hearing lately make me feel just that. All of Paris is talking about your intimacies. Each one is discussed in great detail, savored on the palate like a fine wine. Many people say that you are clinically insane, that you suffer from erotomania. At the same time, a whole other group of stories is circulating about your belligerent acts against the young men you employ as your secretaries and apprentices, and the way you end long friendships with other great men over trifles and misunderstandings.

Finally, and this is perhaps the most damaging, the news

is circulating that you no longer create any works of art. Instead, you draw one sketch after another of young women engaged in the solitary act of giving themselves pleasure.

Of course I am worried by all these rumors. I have known you for twenty-five years now, so I do not think I am boasting when I say that I know you well. I was afraid when you stopped working six years ago. I thought then that I simply grieved for the loss to art. Now I see what I really feared was that if you stopped working, your lust for women would overtake you. It seems that it has.

I know how much I and the other women who have loved you have suffered from this disease of yours. I did not realize you suffered from it too. Forgive me.

1909

Rodin,

I worry about the way you treat your women. Gwen John is an excellent painter. But she suffers over you as I did. She wants a relationship of equals, as I did, and as always, you will not give it to her. I know how unhappy and single-minded she is. I hope it will not destroy her.

I worry less about the American Duchess. She is a shrewd businesswoman, and I know she is making you money by raising the prices of your sculptures. It gives me a particular pleasure to hear that the other members of your circle detest her and spread rumors that she is poisoning you slowly with arsenic now that she has taken over your diet. I am also thrilled to hear that she talks so much it drives everyone crazy, that she dominates the household by playing Gregorian chants much too loud on a gramophone, and that she orders you around, dresses you, and arranges your hair, all as if you were a small child. She is the first woman who has ever been domineering and oblivious enough to degrade you.

1 9 1 0

Rodin,

I am writing to let you know I am fully aware that it was you who prevented Judith Cladel's article praising my work from being published in *La Fronde*.

I am sure that I will prevail in the end and that your true hideousness and vile nature will be shown to the world. But at present I do not have the resources to pay my creditors.

How clever of you to show an *Aurore* in Italy which is not mine (and is furthermore not a good piece of work), attribute it to me, and then arrange for it to win the gold medal. If you were not trying to ruin me, enrage me, and drive me mad, I would applaud this escapade as the supreme practical joke.

1 9 1 3

Monsieur Rodin,

Well, I suppose you think you've finally succeeded in silencing me for all eternity.

I admit this came as quite a surprise. It had occurred to me that after my father died, my sister and mother would immediately execute whatever plan they had already devised to get rid of me, and my brother Paul would acquiesce, pretending to be distressed by it, so his colleagues in the world of letters would not blame him. But since I did not know that my father had died, I was not prepared for this sudden incarceration.

I think it apt that you chose an insane asylum. And it is no mental lapse when I say you chose it. Because, though I am sure my sister and mother were planning some way to end the disgrace they felt in having a sister and daughter who had given herself up to a beast and let him destroy her, I am sure it was you who planted the specific idea in their minds of an asylum in the provinces.

Yes, you chose it well. An asylum is more likely to prevent me from creating art because the cries of these tormented souls will distract me. An asylum in the provinces will prevent my colleagues from coming to my aid. And an asylum is better than a prison or a convent or the family's country home because it discredits me in the most convincing way: it throws doubt upon my ability to create art.

You were quite ingenious in your choice, sir, and I list these ramifications, which I'm sure you thought of in advance, only to prove that I understand what you are about.

I do blame myself for falling in love with you; for believing that since you were a great artist, you could also be a great man; for hoping that the fact you finally loved someone deeply and irrevocably would make you kinder; for deluding myself that since you enjoyed women so much, you would treat them as equals. I blame myself for not ceasing to care when I realized you were a ruthless man who was brutal to women.

After you, I was smart enough never to love completely again, just as you had promised yourself, after your sister, never to give yourself completely again. But where you were able to shut out your mistake, I let it poison me and make me bitter. I blame myself for that.

Finally, I blame myself for letting you get this far in your attempt to destroy me. You, who complain so much about your apprenticeship, had only to fight indifference. You did not have a family and a teacher who were in league together to destroy you.

I blame myself for my lack of cunning and deceit. I should have pretended to you that I had no grand aspirations, and to my family that I was chaste. It is my great failure in life that I could not fool you or them. I was not capable of deceit. For that I can only blame myself.

1913

Rodin,

My doctors have just told me why I have been incarcerated, and I must congratulate you on the evil genius of it. What cunning! To set up sophisticated plots to undermine me and my work, not because you intended to carry out my demise by these obvious machinations, but in order to have me suspect it, so that later you might have me incarcerated for paranoid delusions that you yourself orchestrated.

This is truly brilliant, really too marvelous for words, heady in its genius. If it weren't so completely vile and base, I would be quite delighted by the intricacy of it. And I accused you of not appreciating the precious! Surely this ploy is the most precious imaginable.

I suppose you are so smug that you didn't count on this outcry in the Paris press against my incarceration. I hope you are afraid that this plan is about to backfire and that the world is already discovering what you've done to me. I hope you're living in terror of the fact that instead of silencing me, you have given me a voice.

If I am right and you are really terrified, I want to tell you this: all I ever wanted was to be an artist. I never wanted to hurt you or to reveal what a monster you are. I loved you. I would never have harmed you. So you have brought all this shame down on yourself for trying to harm me.

By reading all the wonderful, true things that are being written about me in the Paris press, I have acquainted myself with the law of 1838, which allows a family member to lock up another family member for life, with only a doctor's certificate, after which only a family member can secure the poor soul's release. I applaud you for making use of this ingenious law and thereby diverting blame from yourself to my family.

Isn't it like me to have forgotten completely about my inheritance? I was underestimating Louise by believing that her only motivation in removing me from the eyes of Parisian society was to protect her good name. But now that I consider it, it seems only fitting that Louise should want my money, too. How clever of you to point out to her how much more dangerous I might have become to her had I received my inheritance and then, no longer destitute, been able to attend the exhibitions of my artwork.

1 9 1 3

Rodin,

I am sure you never stopped to consider how your sons might feel when they learned that you had incarcerated me. I can assure you that they are horrified by this monstrous deed of yours, and that it will alter their opinion of you forever. I hope you can live with that.

They are threatening to denounce you publicly, declare themselves my sons, and have me removed from this asylum immediately so that they might take care of me; but I made them promise not to. Even if they could prove they are my sons, they most probably could not get me released over the protests of my sister, brother, and mother.

I have devised an elaborate system for working here. Your sons must first smuggle the clay in to me. This is not too difficult, since I am still working in miniature and there-fore do not require much. I must work at night so the Sisters will not notice. Many of the madwomen in the asylum are insomniacs, so they have seen me working and tried to warn the Sisters, but the Sisters believe they are just raving. I don't mind working at night—it is easier to concentrate—but I am tired all day. Luckily, the doctors are not suspicious of this. They take it as a good sign—the body's way of healing the mind. Your sons are also assigned the task of smuggling the figures out of the asylum. This is not too difficult, since the figures are so tiny.

Your sons want to take the figures to my dealer, Eugène Blot, to have them exhibited. But as much as I trust Monsieur Blot, it would be extremely dangerous to show the figures now. I fear your and my family's reprisals. I prefer to wait un-til we are all dead, until only my sons remain, and then allow them to exhibit the busts. They are not happy with this plan because they want me released, and they are convinced that an exhibition of my work would prove my sanity. But I am not so much worried about my release now as I am about securing a place for my art in history, and I am convinced that this is the unfortunate choice I am forced to make.

Your sons have agreed to oblige me, even though they disagree. They have plasters made of my maquettes, and when they have money, René has them copied in bronze and François carves them in marble or onyx, which is the material to which they are most suited. You would be proud of your sons; they have become quite dexterous craftsmen—René at enlarging and foundry work, François at stonecutting. And at the same time they manage to continue their studies in law, architecture, and art, while they visit me faithfully and handle my affairs skillfully. I cannot imagine how they do it. They are superlative sons.

I had thought my imprisonment in this asylum would not be much different from the imprisonment of poverty, but of course I was wrong. My poverty was a choice I made for my art. This asylum is not a choice. At the Quai Bourbon I could not go out because I had nothing suitable to wear; here I cannot go out because the doors are locked. There I lived in the company of many independent but affectionate cats and a few curious but harmless neighbors; here I live surrounded by keening women who break my heart.

There, at the Quai Bourbon, I was free to work night and day, my only distraction being my creditors. Here, at the asylum, I am forced to work at night, in secret, smuggling my supplies in and my completed figures out, constantly interrupted by the litanies of these poor women.

At the Quai Bourbon the public was indifferent to me, and my family thought of me as nothing more than a common prostitute because my relations with you did not end in marriage. But my colleagues, some critics and dealers looked upon me as a great artist, the most promising young sculptor in Paris. Now that I am confined to this asylum, I am thought of at best as a victim of my family's retribution. At worst, my very being is questioned, my ability to create art and to live in the world is thrown into doubt.

There are different types of incarceration. Though I did not realize it at the time, of those possible incarcerations poverty was the most benign. And certainly, this asylum must be the most degrading. I am sure that that was your purpose. For it was not enough to get me out of sight; you needed to break my spirit, and my family wished to punish me. A convent, a debtors' prison, sequestration at the family home in Villeneuve—these were not enough to ruin me, and you knew it.

1 9 1 5

Rodin,

I wonder how you feel about this war. I hear that after becoming disenchanted with life in London, you've moved to Rome, where you have made an ice cream parlour into a studio and no one speaks French. Are you bored? Do you sulk because attention has been diverted away from you, because no one comes to visit you or holds banquets in your honor? Or are you concerned about your cathedrals being destroyed? I wonder if you will survive this war.

I have had the privilege of changing residences many times, but I have never had the unique experience of changing asylums. I am being transferred, as you must know, from Ville-Evrard to Montdevergues. They say it is because of the war, but I know it is because you want me to be further from Paris, and you've used the war as an excuse to execute your wishes. I was causing too much trouble for you at Ville-Evrard; it was too easy for me to smuggle letters in and out, to speak with friends who went to the press.

I know you're hoping to discourage me and make it even more difficult for me to obtain my release; but I assure you that this will only make me try harder and put you in even greater danger of exposure.

In the past, when choosing a residence, I chose it for the wildness of the garden (as you did your rooms at the Hôtel Biron), or because the walks in the neighborhood would be pleasant, or because the building itself had some special ar-

chitectural or historical feature (as La Folie Neuborg), or because the rooms seemed well-suited to work. If I were in an
especially capricious mood, I would choose an apartment or
studio for its view.

Now I have no choice. I am being moved once again,
without notice and against my will. My concern now is not for
the garden, the view, the neighborhood, the inspiration, the
architectural features. I am concerned primarily with desperate fundamentals. Will the asylum food make me so sick I will
be forced to subsist on potatoes and eggs I cook myself? Will
the Sisters be abusive or simply silent? Will the other inmates
be more wretched than those at Ville-Evrard? Will I be punished when I am caught smuggling mail in and out of the
asylum, when descriptions of my plight are read in the Paris
press, when friends are caught visiting? These are now my
pathetic concerns.

But I will not give up. Even though they have sent me
further away, I am trying to have myself moved to an asylum
in Paris. I know you will do everything to prevent this because,
if I were in Paris, my friends, colleagues, and the press would
be reminded of my plight. I know your influence is strong, and
I probably won't succeed in having myself moved to Paris. But
I do revel in the crisis it has provoked within my family. They
are all forced to examine their consciences.

In the meantime, the doctors both at Ville-Evrard and here
at Montdevergues have written my mother to inform her that
I am well now and should be removed from their asylum. Of
course, she refuses to release me and she is the only one who
legally can. I am telling you this to prove to you that even the
doctors understand that I am quite sane and am being kept
here for no other reason than vengeance. I have also heard
about your meager fund for my internment, which contributes
500 francs per year to keep me here, about one-sixth the price
of a single bronze copy of *Fugit Amor*. I take this as your way
of saying you wish to keep up a slight pretense of feeling sorry
for me, for those who are stupid enough to believe it, but that

you really intend to gall me by this insipid gesture. When have I ever misread your actions?

1 9 1 7

Rodin,

My sons have told me that you are going to die, and that amidst the chaos which reigns at the Hôtel Biron, Judith Cladel is pushing forward a plan to evict the other artists and transform the house into a museum to exhibit your works. Your sons have also told me that you have requested, should the museum be established, that my room at the Hôtel Biron be used exclusively to show my works. They tell me that Mathias Morhardt supports this plan.

So even on your deathbed you cling to this notion that my artwork should live only in your shadow.

I will write Mlle Cladel and Monsieur Morhardt and emphasize to them once again that I do not wish to exhibit under your auspices, and that doing so would be against my express wishes. I will further suggest that they use that room to exhibit all the works you stole from me (though the room is much too small for that), and to document the criminal way in which I was incarcerated and am being held against my will. Of course, they will refuse to do this.

1 9 1 7

Monsieur Rodin,

So you have died, then. I did not think you would outlive the war. Your youngest son, René, brought me the news. He comes to visit me almost every day. He has told my keepers that he is an art student who worships me and desires to be my apprentice. When François comes to visit, he claims to be René. I do not want my keepers to know that there are two of them. Your sons invented this ruse. They are clever boys, all of twenty-five. They escaped the war because of their shortsightedness and dyspepsia, which they know they inherited from you and for which they are very grateful.

René has told me that on your deathbed you asked for me. I still do not believe him. But François, who was also at the bedside (he was hired on as a marble cutter in your studio to replace the men who had left for the war), claimed you asked for your wife. When one of your circle (who are all sycophants and should be expelled) explained that Rose had died several months before, you became irritable and said it was your wife in Paris you wanted.

I told René that François was mistaken, that there had been so many after me, you were undoubtedly asking for the American Duchess or that English painter. (This is not slander against you; your sons are well aware of your activities.)

But René insisted to me François heard the others around the bedside murmur my name; they all agreed I had been your greatest love, and that it was I you were asking for.

Don't delude yourself. I know why you were calling for me. You wanted to be forgiven for all the sins you committed against me—theft, adultery, prevarication, subjugation, and now this incarceration. Don't think that even on your deathbed I would forgive you. I will never forgive you. And it is not because I have no heart. I do. It is because your crimes are too great to be forgiven.

So, François Auguste René Rodin, creator of so much unhappiness in the world, I wanted to ask you: Are you a different person, now that you are dead? Are you a kinder and better person? Do you see the errors of your ways and all the harm you have inflicted on people?

I wonder if, after we die, or right before, we are able to see our lives and our faults clearly. I look forward to that day when I can see without doubts, questions, and excuses exactly what I did wrong and finally be at peace with this life. I wonder if this happened to you and, if so, what the results were.

1918

Rodin,

I hear the copy of *The Waltz* I gave to Monsieur Debussy has been stolen. Was this crime perpetrated by someone of your circle? Does this mean that even though both of you are dead, you still can't tolerate a former lover possessing a figure of mine? And to think, if I had married Debussy when he had asked me, I would be a respectable widow now, not locked up in an asylum for the insane.

The family is bickering again. My brother Paul has blamed our mother for ruining me by favoring our sister Louise. I wonder how many lives are dominated by this problem. Isn't that everybody's problem really, that at one time long ago we wanted someone to love us who did not love us, or did not love us enough, or did not love us more than someone else, or, in your case, did not love you enough not to die of a broken heart—isn't that your problem with your sister? Now, it seems everything we do is provoked by this lack of love we experienced a long time ago. For example, would you have treated Rose and me so poorly if your sister hadn't died of love for Barnouvin, if you hadn't blamed yourself and promised never to love so completely again? Would I have let you get the upper hand with me if I hadn't been hoping to win that love away from Rose, the way I failed to win my mother's love away from Louise? Would Debussy have loved me if he hadn't been trying to win me away from you? Would Rose have loved you if she hadn't been trying to win you back from models? I wonder if this is not, after all, the root of the problem—our trying over and over to win the love that has been denied us or lost to us.

1926

Rodin,

My nephew tells me that my brother Paul has been made an ambassador. He has purchased the Château de Brangues

137

near Grenoble. My nephew also tells me that when my brother speaks of me, it is as if I were already dead. He uses me as an example of why a person should not choose art as a profession. I wonder if he realizes that he made me an example. After all, if he had not locked me up, I would simply be an artist, working in solitude in the face of public indifference.

1 9 2 9

Rodin,

I am writing to tell you my mother has died and she will soon be joining you in the hell of malice, revenge, jealousy, and hatred against me that was certainly of your own making.

1 9 3 2

Rodin,

I received the kindest letter today from my dealer, Blot. He says that you and I and three or four others of our generation showed greatness and authenticity. So at last we are admired as equals. I told you the day would come.

Monsieur Blot goes on to describe me as a woman of great beauty, mystery, sensuality, and genius. It is good to be remembered this way, since even I have forgotten all, except perhaps the genius. He goes on to tell me you cried over my portrait and that I was the only one you truly loved. I know he says this with good intentions, to flatter me, honor me, and perhaps appease me. I imagine he even believes it is true.

I wonder if it is true. It might be. When you met Rose, you were too young to love. She was beautiful at first and shared your life, but she was really your housekeeper, your model, your studio apprentice. Then I came along. I was young and beautiful, you were forty and about to become successful in your career. Do you ever wonder if it was your love of me that inspired you to make those figures for the colossal doors? That was the spur you needed. You would never have created your *Balzac* without the doors, and you would never have executed the doors without me. Do you think it is not so? I wonder. Already, people are attributing your success to me.

After me, you were famous, and so the women you met then were the rewards of fame and once again inferior.

If you loved me because, at that moment in your life between obscurity and fame, you were in the best position to love, then you loved me most.

But I would not like to think that I was so important because of when you met me, but rather because of who I was and how I treated you. I showed you how to love without surrendering. Isn't that what you wanted after your sister died? I suppose you wanted to love that way and did. But you didn't want to be loved that way.

Monsieur Blot assures me that I have suffered too much on your account, and that nothing could justify your conduct, but that time will put things right. Do you think it will?

1935

Rodin,

Even though you are now almost twenty years in the grave, I am writing to tell you that my work is being exhibited with great prestige and distinction at the Exposition des Femmes Artistes Modernes. I am hoping that perhaps now, when the artists and critics are beginning to soundly reject and even forget your work, mine will finally be able to be noticed. It is not enough for you to die so my art can flourish; it seems your reputation must also die. As much as I despise you and what you've done to me, I must admit that I admire your work and find this unfortunate. But perhaps after my work is recognized and flourishing, your reputation can enjoy a rebirth, and our work can coexist as equals in the world of art, as we should have done as lovers and artists when you were alive and I was not incarcerated.

I am not going to die yet, but I believe that I have finally succeeded in erasing myself. I have tried to grow smaller and smaller in this ludicrous, painful world of the asylum, so that one day I might cease to exist, and at that moment I would finally have some peace.

I think that after many years of effort and discipline, I have finally achieved this. No one looks at me, speaks to me, or even utters my name. I have become invisible. I could probably even work on my sculptures in the daytime now without trouble. But it has become a habit to work at night, and there is no point in changing that now.

This success has brought me peace. I don't know exactly what I have achieved—a different way of seeing, another plane of existence, perhaps. It feels almost mystical, the way the nuns would feel if they were allowed to practice their calling without restraint. It reminds me of those Japanese watercolors I saw so long ago at the exhibit of 1883. The Japanese artists must have felt the way I feel now. This feeling must have been commonplace for them, part of their daily lives. I got an inkling of it then, when I was only twenty. There is something Eastern in this peace. Does this mean I am about to die?

When I was first incarcerated thirty years ago, I was terrified by the idea that the grief might be too much to bear. Now I realize, ironically, that the true horror was that I could bear the grief, and I did bear it. It would have been much easier if I had died of it then.

1943

Rodin,

I am going to die now. I will not be joining you in hell because, as you know, my sins of hubris, martyrdom, bitterness, exaggeration, and the excessive way I cherished my own victimization hurt no one but myself.

I have arranged for my sons to steal my body from the asylum after I die, and bury it under the window of my room at the Hôtel Biron. I am not abdicating to you in doing this. I do not see the Hôtel Biron as a museum for your works, even though that is what it has become. I see it as a house in Paris where, for a brief moment, just a few years, several great artists lived under the same roof and pursued their art. They didn't always agree with each other, sometimes they didn't even like each other, but they respected each other as equals. I want to be a part of that now, even though it is too late.

I have entrusted all my artwork to my sons. I have asked them to reintroduce my work to the public only when they believe the time is right, that is, favorable to the world recognizing me as a great artist, on a par with the other artists of the Hôtel Biron. If, during their lifetimes, this moment in history does not arise, I have asked them to pass this duty down to their own children. For I am in no hurry now to be recognized as a great artist. I know I am one and that someday the world will know. I have plenty of time now. I am sure you understand this. Wasn't it you who said that patience is a form of action?

I have told my sons that I want to be remembered as a student of Alfred Boucher, along with Chagall, Modigliani, and Lipchitz. If I am remembered in connection with you at all, I wish to be remembered as the only woman you really loved, the one whom you betrayed and lost.

The Spiritual Exercises of Vaslav Nijinsky

PURPOSE

The purpose of these exercises is to help the exercitant understand what feeling is.

PARTICULAR EXAMINATION OF CONSCIENCE

As soon as he wakes up in the morning, the exercitant should resolve to understand feeling. After the noon meal he should ask himself what he has felt since waking. He should review each instance. In his review he should ask himself which feelings he failed to understand and how he might allow himself to understand feelings in the future. He should renew his resolve to try again.

After the evening meal the exercitant should repeat his examination for the period from the first examination to the second.

The exercitant should compare each examination period to the previous one, each day to the previous one, and each week to the previous one, noting his improvement.

GENERAL EXAMINATION OF CONSCIENCE

The exercitant should review the difference between the existence of feeling and the lack of feeling. Under the category of feeling he should distinguish among:

> love, affection, sentiment
> passion, fervor, ardor
> excitement, stimulation, exhilaration, titillation
> agitation, perturbation, turbulence
> trepidation, disquiet, restlessness, unrest
> tension, strain, nervousness
> frigidity, coldness, callousness, obliviousness
> heartlessness, spiritlessness, dispassion

The exercitant should remind himself of the difference between lack of feeling and defensiveness, lack of feeling and the appearance of no feeling, lack of feeling and shock, numbness, restraint, etc.

THE EXERCISE PROGRAM

The first exercise should be performed upon waking, the second after lunch, the third after dinner, the fourth before going to bed. If this regimen is too strenuous, the exercitant should perform one exercise each day upon waking.

Other exercises like these four can be devised by using the other emotions discussed in the General Examination of Conscience. The exercitant should simply ask himself the inevitable questions.

The exercitant should continue an exercise until he is no longer learning from the exercise, at which time he should substitute one of his own devising. The exercitant should continue the exercise program until he understands feeling or is no longer learning from the exercises. If the exercitant becomes too exhausted to continue, he should rest for one day, or one week, or whatever period of time he feels is necessary and appropriate, and should begin the exercises again.

FIRST EXERCISE

Remember the first person you ever loved. Imagine her eyes and her hair. Imagine her looking at you. Recreate the moment you realized you loved her. Imagine the room, the weather, the way the light fell. Remember what you said and what she said.

Remind yourself of what you want and desire.

Review your life. Recall to mind each person you have loved, looking upon them year by year, period by period. To help yourself do this, recall to mind the place and house where you lived, the people you knew, the work you performed.

In each instance, imagine the beloved. Imagine his face and hair, his eyes and body. Conjure up his smile and his look of doubt. Imagine a room or a place. Imagine yourselves together in that room. Imagine what he would say to you and you to him.

Do this for each person you have loved. And in relation to each person, consider who you are. Were you older or younger than the beloved? What did the beloved teach you? How did the beloved make you suffer? What were your greatest moments of consolation and desolation? How were you a better person for having loved him? A worse person? What did you learn?

Let yourself be struck with amazement when you consider how your love for this person affected and changed you.

SECOND EXERCISE

Remind yourself of what you want and desire.

Review everything you have seen, heard, smelled, tasted, and touched in the previous exercise. Try to draw some knowledge from this.

Remember the first person with whom you were in love. Imagine her face, her eyes, her body. Imagine her laugh and her anger.

Imagine how you felt when you first realized you were in love with her. Imagine how you felt the first time you touched her. Imagine the way you felt the first time you made love to her. Imagine the way you felt when you knew you would not see her again.

Imagine how you felt when you made love for the last time. See the place where you made love. Imagine its length, depth, and breadth. See her undress and stand before you. Look at the look in her eyes. Look at her looking at you. Hear the cries you both made. Taste the tears, taste the taste of her skin. Sense the touch of you touching her. Sense the touch of her touching you.

Review your life. Recall to mind each person you have been in love with, looking upon them year by year, period by period. To help yourself do this, recall to mind the place and house where you lived, the people you knew, the work you performed. In each instance, imagine the beloved. Imagine his hair and eyes and skin. Imagine his laugh. Imagine him looking at you. Imagine his body against yours. Imagine yourself touching him. Imagine him touching you. Imagine yourselves in a room or a place. What does he say to you? What do you say to him?

For each person with whom you were in love, imagine how you felt about him when you first met. Imagine how you felt when you realized you were in love. Imagine how you felt when you first made love, when you quarreled, when he hurt you, when you knew you couldn't have what you wanted, when you parted. Ask yourself what you gained from being in love with this person. What did you learn? How are you changed? Let yourself be struck with amazement when you consider how your love for this person affected and changed you.

Imagine you are a man in love with another man. Imagine you are a woman in love with another woman. Review each of the people you've been in love with. For each, imagine that person is a man. Imagine he is a woman. Imagine falling in love with that person if you were a man, then if you were a woman, if he were a man, if he were a woman. Imagine you are a child in love with a grownup. Imagine you are a grownup in love with a child.

THIRD EXERCISE

Review everything you have seen, heard, smelled, tasted, and touched in the first two exercises. Try to draw some knowledge from this.

Remember the first time someone you loved died. Imagine how you learned of the loss. Imagine how you felt in the days and weeks that followed. Imagine what the things around you looked like. Imagine what people said to you and what you said. Review your life. Recall to mind each person you have loved who has died, looking upon them year by year, period by period. To help yourself do this, recall to mind the place and house where you lived, the people you knew, the work you performed. In each instance, imagine where you were when you found out. Imagine how you felt. Imagine the days and weeks that followed. Imagine what things looked like then. Imagine what people said to you and what you said. Imagine what you thought about the person you lost. Imagine yourself letting go of that person. Imagine how you felt then. Imagine yourself grieving. Imagine how you grieved.

For each beloved you have lost, ask yourself how that loss affected or changed you. Ask yourself what you have learned.

Remind yourself of what you want and desire.

Let yourself be struck with amazement when you consider how your grief affected and changed you.

Imagine your own death. Imagine the place and the time. Imagine how you will die. Imagine what you will say and who will be there. Imagine whether you are afraid or not afraid.

Imagine your death as you fear it.

Imagine your death as you would like it.

Remember each time you thought you were going to die. For each instance, imagine where you were. Imagine the circumstances that compelled you to believe you would die. Imagine what you thought about. Imagine how you felt when you realized you would not die.

Remember the times you wished you were dead. For each instance, imagine the circumstances. Imagine how you felt. Remember how you imagined your own death. Imagine the moment you stopped wishing for your death. Imagine why and how you stopped wishing.

Remember the times you have wanted other people dead. For each instance, imagine the circumstances. Imagine how you felt. Imagine what you did and said. Imagine how you wished the person dead. Imagine the moment when you no longer wished the person dead.

FOURTH EXERCISE

Remind yourself of what you want and desire.

Review everything you have seen, heard, smelled, tasted, and touched in the previous exercises. Try to draw some knowledge from this.

Remember the first time you had power over another person. Imagine who that person was, what she looked like, how her hair felt, how she looked at you. Imagine what you did and said to dominate her. Imagine what it felt like to dominate her. Imagine if you were kind or cruel when you dominated her.

Review your life. Recall to mind each person you have dominated, looking upon them year by year, period by period.

To help yourself do this, recall to mind the place and house where you lived, the people you knew, the work you performed. In each instance, imagine the person. Imagine how he looked, how his hair felt, how he looked at you. Imagine what you did and said to dominate him. Imagine what it felt like to dominate him. Imagine if you were kind or cruel when you dominated him. Remember the first time someone had power over you. Imagine the person, what she looked like, how her hair felt, how you looked at her. Imagine what she did and said to dominate you. Imagine how you felt. Imagine if she was kind or cruel when she dominated you.

Review your life. Recall to mind each person who has dominated you. To help yourself do this, recall to mind the place and house where you lived, the people you knew, the work you performed.

In each instance, imagine what he looked like, how his hair felt, how you looked at him. Imagine what he did and said to dominate you. Imagine how you felt. Imagine if he was kind or cruel when he dominated you.

Imagine the people you would like to dominate. For each person, imagine what he would look like, how his hair would feel, how he would look at you. Imagine what you would do when you dominated him. Imagine if you would be cruel or kind when you dominated him.

Imagine the people you would like to have power over you. For each person, imagine what he would look like, how his hair would feel, how he would look at you. Imagine what he would do to dominate you. Imagine how you would feel. Imagine if he would be cruel or kind when he dominated you.

For each instance above, imagine how the person would feel when you dominated him or were dominated by him.

Remember what you desire.

Let yourself be struck with amazement when you consider how your power over other people and their power over you has affected and changed you.

FEBRUARY 1906

I don't plan to stay in Paris forever, but I'm glad I've come back for a second visit. As much as I enjoyed my success doing portrait photography in New York, I confess it frightened me. I felt as if my work were stagnating. I do believe it is possible to use photography for both art and practical matters like portraits, but I also believe that I need to continue to move forward. I wasn't doing that anymore, so I came back here to Paris, where six years ago, at the age of twenty-one, I discovered so much about art. I hope I can do that again; then this visit to Paris can be a rejuvenation of my spirit that will sustain me when I return to New York.

MARCH 1906

I went to visit the great master Rodin, who was so kind to me six years ago when I first visited him at Meudon. I told him about Stieglitz's new 291 Gallery in New York, and how we would like him to be the first to exhibit there. He was flattered and told me I could send whatever I chose. I explained to him that the gallery was small, and that I would need to send drawings and watercolors.

JANUARY 1907

Since I had told Rodin that the first exhibit at the 291 would be his work, I was horrified to learn that Stieglitz opened the gallery with a show of Pamela Coleman's watercolors. I was extremely disappointed but also worried that Rodin might take offense. He has rejected several friends lately as the result of misunderstandings such as this one.

JUNE 1907

I borrowed a Goerzanschutz Klapp camera from a friend yesterday, thinking that I would take up documentary reportage, and headed off to the horse races at Longchamps, filled with purpose. I was surprised to find, however, that the people who go to the horse races here are not so much interested in the races as they are in showing off the latest fashions, in seeing each other and being seen. I took some good pictures, but I had to revise my intentions before doing so.

A company called Lumière has introduced something they've named autochrome plates, which produce color photographs. The results are amazing and the process is relatively simple. Stieglitz was here briefly on his way to the Alps, and I had the chance to show him some of the experiments I had made with the new process. He was astounded and took some plates with him.

AUGUST 1907

I have been to London, where I photographed George Bernard Shaw. He is a delightful man, so puckish and whimsical. I used some of the color plates because I hoped they might complement his complexion (blond-red hair and beard). Stieglitz likes the results so much that he wants to publish them in *Camera Work*.

DECEMBER 1907

I have taken a room in a big house called the Hôtel Biron. It is a seventeenth-century mansion, which was originally built for a duke, was for some time a convent, and has recently been given over to the French state. While the government decides what to do with it, they are renting the rooms out very cheaply to artists. Henri Matisse holds painting classes in a building near the chapel and also has a room downstairs in the main house, where he works and sometimes stays. A young Spanish painter named Picasso also has a room here, though his main studio, the Bateau Lavoir, is located in Montmartre. A sculptress named Clara Westoff was living here in an upstairs room facing the garden, but she has returned to Germany, and her husband, the poet Rainer Maria Rilke, is staying in her studio. Rilke used to be Rodin's amanuensis and has written two monographs on the master. Picasso has recently convinced the primitive painter Henri Rousseau to live here. Picasso found one of Rousseau's portraits in a junk shop and greatly admires the older man, who seems very lively and good-natured.

1908

Rousseau is sulking over Apollinaire's review of his work at the Salon des Indépendants. Rousseau says Apollinaire recognizes and praises every other artist of genius except him. He says the review is condescending and incorrect. He insists he must not lose his ingenuousness as Apollinaire warns he must, that no artist knows exactly where he is going or what he wants, so there is no point in singling out Rousseau on that score, and that he does have pride but also modesty.

FEBRUARY 1908

I had been unsuccessful in trying to persuade Matisse to agree to exhibit at the 291, so I enlisted Sara Stein to encourage him. As the result of her coaxing, Matisse has agreed to exhibit. I've been having a similar problem convincing Picasso, so Gertrude Stein has agreed to speak to him in my behalf.

MARCH 1908

Matisse will be exhibiting at the 291 this month. It will be his second show outside of France—the first one was in London in January. He is very pleased about it, now that he has agreed to do it. He came up to my room tonight to ask me for details about the gallery, and also how I thought the Americans would react to his work. Matisse introduced Picasso to a Russian art dealer named Shchukin, who has purchased several of Picasso's paintings. Shchukin says he will stop by every few months, and Matisse claims he is a man of his word. Shchukin said Matisse and Picasso are the best painters of their generation.

Jean Cocteau, a young poet who is determined to distinguish himself at all costs, has just rented out the sacristy and decorated it with goat skins. If any visitor to his new bachelor apartment looks askance at them, he will snatch one up, inhale its scent, and with great theatrical fervor exclaim that he adores the smell of furs.

Cocteau says the Hôtel Biron reminds him of the Hôtel Pimodan on the Ile St-Louis, where Baudelaire used to live. I think he aspires to become one of the Decadents. In order to achieve this aim, he invites Catulle Mendès to come to his rooms to recite poetry and Reynaldo Hahn to sing Venetian ballads. He believes in this manner he pays homage to the Baudelarian reception.

Cocteau, in his impatience to be famous and loved by great men, insists he wants to meet Rilke but is afraid of coming inside the main house. Rilke, for his part, wanders around the house in a trance and doesn't speak to anyone. He is working on a prose piece entitled *The Notebooks of Malte Laurids Brigge*. Sometimes he refers to it as a novel, sometimes as memoirs. I believe if Cocteau tried to introduce himself, Rilke would dismiss him as impertinent. This sounds unfair, since Rilke himself has sought out great men in Tolstoy and Rodin and should understand the impulse. But he wouldn't reject Cocteau out of insensitivity. He would reject him because he is working. He works in long sprints, without resting, for weeks or months at a time, and when he does, it is as if he were caught up in a whirlwind. Nothing can touch him.

1 9 0 8

Rousseau says there are ghosts in the house. At night I can hear him chasing them and swatting at them with magazines and paint rags. He says that when he worked for the Municipal Toll Service, he used to shoot at them. When I asked him why he didn't just leave the ghosts alone and let them live in the house with us, he said it is because they ridicule him with foul smells and keep him awake at night.

I suppose I shouldn't be surprised that so many women come to visit Rousseau. He is good-looking, and I would imagine his ingenuousness is charming. He loves these women while they visit and asks each one to marry him, but they refuse. When they leave, he goes right back to his painting, as if nothing had happened. I think the difference between Rousseau and Rodin is that Rousseau does not use women for inspiration, he doesn't seek them out, he doesn't mind when they refuse him marriage, and he doesn't seem to miss them when they're gone. Unlike Rodin, he doesn't mix with high society. As a result, Rousseau seems to suffer much less over women, even though he is just as popular.

Picasso is working less at night now so that he can receive visitors. The poet Max Jacob and critic Apollinaire come by most often. No one disturbs him in the morning except those innocents who don't know he sleeps late.

I was invited into Picasso's rooms yesterday while some other people were also visiting and noticed his Sherlock Holmes and Buffalo Bill novels. When he caught me looking at them, he explained that he likes adventure stories.

1 9 0 8

Rousseau has started to throw his own art parties. He holds them on Saturday nights. He sends out formal invitations that list what events will take place at the party, like a theater program. He dresses up in a dark, high-buttoned suit with a rosette in his buttonhole and wears a large beret over his white hair. He relies on a cane, except when he plays the fiddle for his guests. He arranges chairs all facing front to a makeshift stage, greets his guests at the door and seats them in the order of their arrival. His students play their instruments or recite poetry. His guests are allowed to perform.

These parties are becoming fashionable. Apollinaire and Delaunay often come, Picasso and Braque come, Max Jacob often comes. These painters seem in awe of how much fun the old man can have and still paint such amazing pictures.

1 9 0 8

I am not sure what to think of this banquet Picasso gave in Rousseau's honor. I know Picasso truly respects Rousseau and his paintings, but so many of Picasso's friends have ridiculed Rousseau and played tricks on him, taking advantage of his childlikeness, that I'm suspicious of them. But Rousseau did have a good time. I think he knows when people are making fun of him, and it's possible that Picasso's sentiments dominated the party, despite what some of the guests felt. Picasso put Rousseau in a special raised seat at the head of the table, hung Chinese lanterns around his studio (he held the party at the Bateau Lavoir in Montmartre), and decorated the Rousseau portrait he'd recently bought with streamers.

Marie Laurencin got drunk for a change. Apollinaire brought Rousseau, who brought his violin. The guests, primarily Spaniards and poets, sang songs to Rousseau and recited toasts in his honor. Laurencin and Apollinaire got into a fight, and Gertrude Stein had to settle it. Afterward, Apollinaire sulked in the corner and pretended to write letters. Then Cremintz and Salmon ate soap so they'd foam at the mouth and faked an attack of delirium tremens to scare Miss Stein, but she only thought they were brawling. Rousseau pretended hot wax was not dripping on his bald spot from the Chinese lantern above his seat, and Miss Stein took him home when he started dozing.

JUNE 1908

Picasso has left to spend the remainder of the summer in La Rue des Bois. People in the house say he's despondent over his friend Weigel's suicide. Apparently this is the second close friend of Picasso's to kill himself.

AUGUST 1908

Rodin asked me to photograph his *Balzac* by moonlight at Meudon. I spent an entire night at it, experimenting with different exposures. Some of the negatives look interesting, but I plan to wait and show Rodin prints. The morning after the all-night photography session I found two thousand francs under my breakfast plate. That's about four hundred dollars. I protested that this was too much for a night's work, but Rodin waved me off as impertinent.

LATE AUGUST 1908

Rodin loves the prints of his *Balzac* that I showed him. He says people might eventually understand the sculpture through my photographs. I am very flattered.

SEPTEMBER 1908

Stieglitz bought a set of *Balzac* prints. He says it's the best thing I've done.

SEPTEMBER 3, 1908

Rodin had lunch today with Rilke in Rilke's wife's upstairs rooms. Rilke quoted Beethoven, gave Rodin a wooden St. Christopher, and argued with him about the role of women. Then they effected a reconciliation. They had quarreled several months ago when Rilke was working as Rodin's amanuensis and wrote letters in his own behalf to Rodin's colleagues, which angered Rodin.

The end result of all this is that Rodin has rented the lower rooms on the right back corner of the Hôtel Biron, and Rilke is taking over his wife's rooms, since she will not be returning.

But Rilke did not succeed in convincing Rodin of the ability of woman to transcend desire. Rilke even dragged out his translation of *The Letters of a Portuguese Nun* as proof, but to no avail. Rodin is convinced that women are an obstruction and a trap, but at the same time necessary as an elixir. He refuses to be convinced that they can be equals, artists, transcendent, though he claims he would like to believe it. Rilke was very discouraged by Rodin's attitude and blames it on his race!

SEPTEMBER 1908

Rodin has a cold. Instead of working, he reads Plato, writes his thoughts down on scraps of paper, and sends them sailing across the room in all directions the way he does his quick drawings from the model.

LATE FALL 1908

Picasso has returned from La Rue des Bois and has been spending a lot of time with his friend Braque. A few weeks ago he decided Braque should get married and arranged to introduce him to the daughter of the owner of Le Néant, a cabaret near his Bateau Lavoir studio in Montmartre. They brought Max Jacob and some other poets with them, dressed up in top hats, cloaks, and canes, and arrived at the cabaret. The owner and his daughter were impressed until Picasso and his group drank too much and started clowning around in their usual way. The owner asked them to leave, and they took the wrong top hats and capes on their way out. Now they're afraid to return them.

OCTOBER 1908

Stieglitz is very excited about the Matisse, Picasso, and Rodin exhibits at the 291. He wrote me that he would like to publish an issue of *Camera Work* that would consist of articles written exclusively by the artists who live at the Hôtel Biron.

He wants to exclude articles by writers, so I asked everyone except Cocteau and Rilke. Picasso says he wants to write about what's happening on the Paris art scene. Matisse isn't sure what to do. He thinks he might like to write brief biographies of the artists here at the Hôtel Biron. Rilke doesn't mind being excluded, but he said he might write some poems about the garden at the Hôtel Biron. Cocteau is hurt and says he is planning to write a play in which the tenants of the Hôtel Biron talk to each other. He says it will be so incredible that Stieglitz will feel obliged to include it. I think for my article I might edit these notebooks and submit them.

NOVEMBER 1908

Rodin has offered Camille Claudel the use of one of his rooms here at the house. Since they have not really been friends now for ten years, I doubted she would use it at all, but she does occasionally come and sit in it and stare out the window overlooking the garden. More often, though, she stands outside the house and looks in the windows. When she does come in the house, some of the artists here try to engage her in conversation, especially Rilke, who seems very sympathetic toward her and asks her about her work. I asked her if she would like to contribute something to the tenants of the Hôtel Biron issue of *Camera Work* and explained to her what it was. She said she had been writing some letters to Rodin that she planned never to give him, and she thought these might be appropriate for the magazine!

Cocteau went to a party at the Baron de Pierreborg's with his companion, Maurice Rostand (son of the famous *Cyrano* author, of course—who else?). Maurice and Cocteau were admiring the Decadents, as is their wont, in particular, Aubrey Beardsley, when Paul Claudel overheard. Paul is Camille's younger brother. The tenants of the Hôtel Biron have nicknamed him "The Catholic Puritan of Letters." He happens to be in Paris between diplomatic appointments. Anyway, Mr. Claudel couldn't let this admiration pass without condemning it, and he whispered in a loud voice so Maurice and Cocteau could hear (so apparently everyone could hear) that men of their ilk should be ostracized. Maurice shot back: But who would come to the salons?

Cocteau told us the story in the presence of Camille, and she laughed louder than the rest, the kind of forced laughter that makes people uncomfortable. I think it reassures her that people realize what a prig her brother is and how insensitive to art. But I believe she loves him, and it hurts her that he disapproves of her profession. I also think she must resent the fact that her brother does so well with such little effort, both at literature and in the foreign service, while she works so hard and is still only recognized in the most esoteric art circles. I hear she blames it on Rodin, but I believe she'd be more correct if she blamed her heartache on Rodin and the limited success of her career on her sex. There are such good women artists, and yet so few get any recognition (except perhaps the dancers and actresses), and when they do, they're looked upon as freaks of nature, women who have somehow defied or transcended their sex.

DECEMBER 1908

Our dear Mr. Rousseau is planning one of his famous parties for Max Weber, the young painter who has befriended him. Rousseau assures me that he is inviting a lot of Americans to the party, but he refers to anyone who is not French as an American, so there is really no telling what range of foreigners will be represented.

JANUARY 1909

Rousseau is on trial for forgery and embezzlement. One of his students put him up to it. The defense lawyer is trying to prove his innocence by showing that he is too naïve to have suspected his student of any wrongdoing. To do this, the lawyer is reading excerpts from Rousseau's scrapbook of press clippings and showing his jungle paintings to the jury.

This creates a carnival atmosphere in the courtroom, and the newspapers are capitalizing on the festivities, but the jury seems sympathetic.

Since Rousseau made no financial gain from the embezzlement (the student kept all the money), this fact seems the most compelling way to prove his innocence. But the lawyer seems to be reaching for more theatrical effects. I wish there were some way to protect Rousseau from ridicule, but he doesn't seem to mind it. He treats it as superfluous, the way a wise man disregards gossip.

END OF JANUARY 1909

Rousseau was given a suspended sentence. He's very pleased, has offered to paint a portrait of the judge's wife, and has invited his defense lawyer to his Saturday parties.

1909

The Friends of the Louvre Society gave a tour of the Hôtel Biron today. It regularly gives tours of historic buildings, and since the state is considering restoring it, we were on the Society's list. We were notified in advance of the tour, so we were all able to be on our best behavior (that is, Cocteau wasn't in the midst of throwing a wild party, Rodin refrained from drawing women in erotic poses, Rilke kept his windows shut and did not recite yesterday's work to the garden at the top of his voice, Matisse managed to keep his pupils from imitating his style when copying the plaster model, and Miss Claudel was nowhere to be found). I was quite proud of us, and everything was going along smoothly until the tour headed into the sacristy and discovered Cocteau living there.

In addition to the sacrilege involved, Mrs. Cocteau, Jean's mother, is a member of the Society and was one of the ladies conducting the tour. Evidently, she had no idea that Cocteau had rented a "bachelor's" apartment here. Of course, she was horrified by all the bohemian implications, but she managed to squelch her horror for the duration of the visit and was very diplomatic, while everyone sat on rattan chairs and sofa in Jean's room, ate cakes, drank orangeade off his packing crates, and admired the lilies and doves Matisse had recently painted on the walls in preparation for Jean's next party. But a few hours after the tour was over, Mrs. Cocteau returned to tell her son Jean what she thought of the scandal. She's threatening to cut off his allowance if he doesn't give up the rooms.

1 9 0 9

I was wandering around downstairs this morning and found Rodin's new secretary, Maurice Baud, going through the pockets of all the trousers and jackets Rodin has worn in the last few days. The master changes clothes at least three times a day, so this is a gargantuan task. Mr. Baud must have thought me suspicious, because he was very eager to explain to me that Rodin leaves all his receipts, invoices, and checks in his pockets, in armchairs, on modeling stands, etc., and many have been lost. At present he was searching for a check for fifty thousand francs that had arrived yesterday from America. Rodin could remember the check itself but not where he had put it.

Cocteau is circulating through the main house, trying to solicit poems and drawings for his new magazine, *Schéhérazade*, but no one wants to contribute. Cocteau claims it is the first deluxe magazine for poets, but everyone here is skeptical. Rodin has seen the first issue and does not like its Art Nouveau style, which he calls the "internationalist" style. He also dislikes the fact that the magazine says it is published here at the Hôtel Biron. When he confronted Cocteau with this tidbit, Cocteau said, But I am the publisher! and Rodin went back to his erotic sketches. Cocteau left with a flourish, saying that Bonnard's drawings would appear in the next issue and Rodin would be envious.

MARCH 1909

Rousseau is trying to get everyone in the house to write letters to his new girlfriend, Léonie, attesting to his stature as a painter and to his good character. Apparently, Léonie won't marry him, but he is not about to forget about her the way he has about the other ladies who visit him. Léonie is a clerk in the Bon Marché and clearly doesn't know what to think of Rousseau. Rousseau wanders around the house pouting and playing his violin. He's still painting, but I am afraid that it will all end badly.

MAY 18, 1909

The preview (dress rehearsal) for the opening of the Russian Imperial Ballet at the Théâtre du Châtelet was held today. Diaghilev completely renovated the theater for the occasion. The high society of the Paris art world was invited, as were journalists. Cocteau is sulking because he wasn't invited. He claims Diaghilev feels threatened that he, Cocteau, might steal Nijinsky away from him. Cocteau insists that Diaghilev would not be jealous if Cocteau were not so irresistible. At present Cocteau is plotting ways to be introduced into the ballet company's inner circle. I'm sure he will succeed.

1909

Rodin has taken his student Malvina Hoffman to the Louvre this evening for what he calls "The Candle Test." He performs this ritual for one of his students at least twice a month. Miss Hoffman says he takes her at closing time, and holds the lighted candle up to one of the Egyptian sculptures so she can see the shadows reflected by the contours. While he moves the light along the sculpture, he discourses on the beauty of the ancients.

Apollinaire challenged Max Daireaux to a duel because he felt insulted by Daireaux's review of his poems. Then he asked Picasso to help him out of the mess. On the day of the duel,

Picasso hid Apollinaire in his Bateau Lavoir studio while Max
Jacob, dressed in a top hat, tails, and monocle, acted as a
go-between among the seconds, who were installed in two
nearby cafés. Max Jacob managed to get both sides drunk, and
then drew up a document which both groups signed.

Cocteau and Picasso were in Rodin's rooms, admiring his
Greek and Egyptian artifacts. They were trying to discern
which ones were real, which fake, and which contraband, but
neither knows enough about it to judge. Picasso says the Greek
drinking cup was made in the nineteenth century and the
Tanagra figures are fake, but he concedes the charm of the
copies and understands why Rodin would want to collect them
even though he can't verify their authenticity. Rodin himself
conceded that the Hermes statuette is a fake and can be
bought for a few francs in a plaster cast dealer's shop in Montparnasse. Then he looked dismayed and victimized for a moment. When he does catch the swindlers, he buys the pieces
anyway, but that much cheaper.

Picasso is a collector of African sculpture and jewelry. He
wants Fernande to wear the jewelry, but it makes her self-
conscious. Picasso asked Rodin many questions about how he
approaches dealers and how he determines whether a piece is
real or fake, so he could apply these lessons to his own collecting. But since Rodin doesn't worry too much about authenticity and buys what he likes for the sheer pleasure of it, he
couldn't help Picasso very much.

Picasso has gone back to Spain for the summer. People in
the house say he's homesick.

NOVEMBER 1909

I spent part of the summer at Voulangis, where the
painter John Marin came to visit me. I convinced him to try my
color box, and I sent the results to the 291 for his most recent
show. Now the critics say he's influenced by Matisse, when it
was really my color box!

The American Duchess bought Rodin a phonograph,

which she winds up for him, and some recordings of Gregorian
chants, which Rilke claims that until now only the Pope possessed. Rodin didn't know what to make of the music until
Rilke said it was beautiful. Rilke says the purpose of the Duchess is to bring Rodin back down from the heights of his art.
Miss Camille Claudel agrees with Rilke with an almost malicious glee. Rilke has mixed feelings about it—he believes it is
both necessary and unfortunate.

FALL 1909

Picasso exhibited the new paintings he did in Spain
this summer. The show was held at the Vollard Gallery and
was a great success. He sold so many paintings that he moved
out of the Bateau Lavoir (though he will retain it to work, and
will keep his room here at the Hôtel Biron), and into a studio
and apartment in Montparnasse. The new place is so big and
luxurious compared to the Bateau Lavoir that Fernande says
she feels anxious and uncomfortable there. They even have a
maid in uniform to serve meals, and have begun to hold their
own Sunday afternoon receptions instead of relying on the
hospitality of the Steins.

A controversy is raging at the Hôtel Biron over whether
or not Picasso should be allowed to bring his pets over from
his Bateau Lavoir and Montparnasse studios. He has cats,
dogs, a tortoise, and a monkey. The Duchess detests the tortoise and monkey, but everyone else wishes *she* would leave.
Rodin is trying to be diplomatic and please everyone.

Picasso congratulated Matisse on the new Apollinaire article that just appeared about him, but Matisse shrugged it off,
saying that he was embarrassed by the article because it made
him sound like a snob.

1 9 0 9

When Rodin met Lou Andreas-Salomé and her friend Ellen Key, he pressed Ellen Key's hand and said with great exuberance, "I know very well, madame, that you were Nietzsche's mistress!" Everyone was embarrassed except Rodin, who seemed quite pleased with the meeting. I do not know if afterward anyone told Rodin that it was Salomé, not Key, who had been Nietzsche's friend, but I am certain someone had explained this to him beforehand.

1 9 1 0

Picasso is installing an exotic bathroom in the sacristy so that he can stage a series of Roman parties.

Matisse came up to my room this evening and asked me to come down and look at something in his studio—he wouldn't tell me what. He seemed very agitated. When we got down to his studio, Matisse stood me in front of *The Dance*, a painting of five vermilion figures dancing in a circle on an emerald lawn against a cobalt background. The figures in the painting seemed to be actually moving.

I explained the Purkinje effect to Matisse, in which warm and cool colors change their values at twilight. I did not feel this was really an adequate response to the genius of his color selection, which in my mind was what had transformed his painting. I was about to add this, but he put his hand on my arm to stop me. He didn't want to know any more. Later I realized why. Though the effect of light on colors might seem a dry, inadequate, and overly scientific explanation to me, it was perfect for Matisse. After all, the Impressionists had insisted that light was what mattered. Matisse had gone off in his own direction, yet here was a photographer telling him his use of color was intuitively correct—it had engaged the light to create vibrancy and movement.

For once, I had said the right thing. For once, the scientific answer was also the aesthetic answer. We were both so pleased that Matisse gave me his painting called *Collioure Rooftops* and I accepted it. He also let me roam around his studio and look at his new work before returning to my own room.

What he's doing really is amazing. He uses pure color, the brightest ones he can find, and chooses the most astonishing ones. Then he applies them to figure or landscape, not according to nature, but according to some more appropriate inner plan or scheme which is more suited to the painting. So, for example, a bather might be rose madder or cerulean blue, the ocean might be ochre. Once the viewer accepts the fact that these colors are not laid out according to nature but according to the forms and groupings in the painting, the rightness and expressive power of the colors is overwhelming. No one else is doing such compelling work; no one understands better the relations among color, form, and content.

1 9 1 0

Picasso took some of the people in the Hôtel Biron over to the Jardin des Plantes. He is friends with the curator's son, who lets him in and shows him the exotic animals. Picasso says he would like to have some tropical birds of his own.

Rilke is railing about the fact that the American Duchess took Rodin to hear Caruso at the Trocadéro. He feels it's demeaning and absurd to expose Rodin to fashionable society. She has also taken him to the ballet, the opera, and the horse races at Longchamps. It is not just the fashionable society and the activities Rilke objects to; it's the way the Duchess curls Rodin's hair (which he has grown out for her), and dresses him in a velvet beret and gloves the color of butter. Rilke feels she takes Rodin so far out of his nature that she makes him ridiculous. Rilke believes that an artist should not try to make himself belong socially by changing his dress or his companions.

Max Weber bought several of Rousseau's paintings two years ago, before he left for New York. Now he plans to exhibit

them at the 291. It will be Rousseau's first one-man show. He's
thrilled. I wish I had arranged it myself as I did the Matisse,
Rodin, and Picasso shows at the 291.

1 9 1 0

Cocteau has taken to his bed with an attack of neurasthenia and won't receive anyone. He is driving the concierge
crazy. In the meantime, his new book of poems, *The Frivolous
Prince,* has just been released, and everyone is trying to contact
him. A copy is circulating through the house here. Rilke
handed it to me without a word. But someone has earmarked
the page where one of Cocteau's "Sonnets to the Hôtel Biron"
appears. Cocteau is currently chasing after that reptile, Count
Robert de Montesquiou, and the sonnet is supposed to make
reference to him.

I don't understand why great poets like Rilke and poets
who could be great, like Cocteau, are always prostrating themselves before older men who are either great artists or men of
position. Why do they do it? Don't they have any pride? Is it
the exuberance of youth? Rodin never did it. Matisse didn't do
it. And it's not just the fact of it that troubles me. It's the way
they debase themselves flattering these men, imitating them,
worshipping at their altars; and these lizards invariably reject
them or somehow brutalize them in the meantime. I don't
understand it. Apparently, Cocteau is madly in love with this
half-baked Count (his mother is a stockbroker's daughter—
hardly the aristocracy), and the Count just sees this young boy
whom everyone praises as a threat, so of course he rejects him
and calls him a young upstart.

Of course, he is a young upstart. But why does this sce-
nario keep repeating itself between young artists of potential
and older men of standing? Does it happen in New York?

1 9 1 0

Rodin returned from his rue de l'Université studio this
afternoon with good news—the flood ruined his Steinway

piano but did not damage the maquette of his *Whistler* monument. He said it was an odd sensation to find some of his drawings floating in water, but none of the work was damaged. Then he began to discourse on the benevolence of Nature.

An interesting development has arisen out of Matisse's show at the 291 this year. Mrs. George Blumenthal, the wife of the director of the Metropolitan Museum in New York, purchased three Matisse drawings for the museum. This is the first time Matisse's work has been acquired for a museum, and Matisse is thrilled about it. I'm pleased the transaction was brought about through the 291.

1910

Cocteau, in his ever-ingenious plan to draw closer to Nijinsky, has just published *Vaslav Nijinsky, Six Poems by Jean Cocteau, Six Drawings by Paul Iribe*, as an answer to Diaghilev, who tries to prevent Cocteau from helping Nijinsky with his showers and rubdowns. Diaghilev likes the publicity but continues his suspicious supervision of Cocteau.

MARCH 1910

Rousseau is moping again over Apollinaire's review of his painting in this year's Salon des Indépendants. Rousseau says Apollinaire has no end of praise for Matisse for "freeing himself from Impressionism" but will only concede that Rousseau's painting, which is a total departure from Impressionism, will be liked by the other painters this year. When Picasso (who is a friend of Apollinaire) suggested it didn't matter what Apollinaire thought, that Rousseau was to be the precursor of many young painters and someday everyone would realize it, Rousseau said he was wrong, that everything that happened in the Paris art world in the next ten years depended on what Apollinaire wrote about it, and that painters' careers would be made or broken based upon what Apollinaire wrote about them. Picasso tried to refute this, but Rousseau would have none of it; he just went into his room to paste Apollinaire's article in his scrapbook and write his rebuttal to it in the margin, as he does with all the press clippings about his work. Picasso went off down the hallway, grumbling that Paris is full of painters who care too much about what critics think of them.

APRIL 10, 1910

Rilke has finished *The Notebooks of Malte Laurids Brigge.* He is leaving for Rome.

JUNE 1910

Rodin went to a testimonial banquet to celebrate his promotion to Grand Officer in the Legion of Honor. Many of his friends are peeved with him for accepting the award, including Rilke, but three hundred people attended the banquet.

I postponed my trip to Voulangis this summer so I could see Stieglitz when he stopped in Paris on his way to Austria. I introduced him to the Steins and to Vollard. We visited the exhibition of Cézanne watercolors at the Bernheim-Jeune Gallery, and Stieglitz liked it so much that we asked to show it at the 291. It's been arranged for next winter, but they only agreed because we've exhibited Matisse and Rodin.

Picasso has left for Cadaques on the Catalonian coast with Fernande and the painter Derain.

AUGUST 1910

Camille Claudel has not used her room in the Hôtel Biron at all this summer or last. There is a rumor circulating through the Hôtel Biron that she leaves Paris for the entire summer and spends it in Tours, where she has two sons, aged fifteen and sixteen. The sons are assumed to be Rodin's, though he denies their existence. So does Miss Claudel. Another rumor has been circulating that before Miss Claudel leaves for Tours at the beginning of the summer, she destroys all the sculptures she has made the previous year. Since she works at her studio on the Quai Bourbon and not here at the Hôtel Biron, there is no way to confirm this.

AUTUMN 1910

In his review of this year's Salon d'Automne in *Poésie*, Apollinaire boasts of having always championed Matisse. This is true, but there is something about his bringing our attention to the fact that embarrasses me. In his defense, I can say that he mentioned something about the decorative power of Matisse's work, and I think that is a crucial point—I believe it is the decorative aspect of his work that makes it both important and underrated.

AUTUMN 1910

Picasso arrived back in Paris from Cadaques two days ago, but it took him that long to reach the house from the train station. Apparently, some of his friends met him at the station, and they stopped in so many cafés and studios along the way that he has only arrived this afternoon.

SEPTEMBER 1, 1910

We had to take Rousseau to the hospital today. He cut his leg and didn't tell anyone about it, and we're afraid blood poisoning has set in.

SEPTEMBER 4, 1910

Rousseau died of the blood poisoning in his leg. The hospital listed his cause of death as alcoholism. The bastards. Everyone knows it could have been prevented.

1910

The composer Erik Satie has rented Rousseau's room here at the Hôtel Biron. It seems that no one has seen much of him in twelve years, and he hasn't published or performed any new music. The word around the house is that he is friends with Debussy and had to get away from him and his music for a while, so he moved to the suburbs of Arceuil-Cachan (he calls it Arcachan) and didn't tell anyone where he went. He rented a room with no heat or water above a café called The Four Chimneys.

Now he's back. There are all sorts of stories circulating around the house about his twelve years of seclusion. They say that he was drinking heavily. They say he used to wear grey velvet corduroy jackets. Now he wears dark suits. They say he carried a hammer in his pocket for protection when he walked in from Arceuil to Montmartre to play piano (that's how he earned his living). Now he leaves a lit clay pipe in his pocket. They say he went back to music school five years ago. He's forty-five! Whatever he did, it worked. Ravel and Debussy are playing his music, and everyone is going wild over it.

There's something so exciting to me about an artist making a comeback after he's been quiet for several years. I almost like it more than the thrill of an older artist finally getting recognition, like Rousseau or Rodin. I'm not sure why I feel this way. Perhaps I sympathize with what the comeback artist has lost and regained, or admire the courage that it must take to face the failure and reemerge from it, as opposed to the unrecognized artist, who has nothing to lose and can only hope for the future. But I'm afraid that I have no sympathy for a young artist who is already successful the way so many are today. I know they work hard and may deserve the recognition, yet it seems somehow shallow and unearned. Maybe I am just a romantic.

I asked Satie if he would like to write something for our issue of *Camera Work*. He showed that twinkle in his eye and asked me if the article could be loosely related to art. I said it could, that Matisse's would be. He said he would work on it in his leisure time. What leisure time?

NOVEMBER 1910

Rilke is back from Rome and is making us all suffer now that after *Malte Laurids Brigge* he seems unable to write anything. He wanders around the house spouting aphorisms; he visits perfume shops and comes back reeking of geranium oil. He is even further depressed by the death of Tolstoy. He is leaving again, this time for Algiers and Tunisia, in the hope that a change of scenery will help him write again.

DECEMBER 20, 1910

Picasso is calling Braque "Wilbur." This puzzled me, so I started asking around the Hôtel Biron about it. No one understood the joke except Matisse, who says Picasso is alluding to Wilbur Wright. Apparently, he feels Mr. Wright's flying machine is the perfect example of a Cubist object.

An exhibit of Picasso's early work opened at the Vollard Gallery today. There was something very rustic and ingenuous about the entire affair. No invitations to the opening reception were sent out, no catalogue was issued for the show, and the pictures were unframed. I suppose this corresponds to Picasso's distaste for exhibitions. When he greets fellow painters, he never asks them where they are exhibiting, or who is representing them, or if they have sold any work. He only asks: Are you working? How is the work going? What are you working on?

DECEMBER 1910

Agnes Meyer, a reporter from the *New York Sun*, wants to start a contemporary magazine called *291* to complement the gallery. She, Stieglitz, and de Zayas have established themselves as the editorial board. Mrs. Meyer is also sponsoring a show of Brancusi marbles at the 291.

WINTER 1911

The Cézanne watercolor exhibit at the 291 has drawn an incredible amount of outrage and criticism, the most we've ever had. Of course, those familiar with contemporary art think it's the best we've ever shown. Some of the visitors to the gallery did notice the fake Cézanne I painted for the exhibit.

They felt it was much more literal than his other work. People even asked to buy it. I'm terrified, and I've asked Stieglitz to burn it immediately. I won't rest until I hear that he has.

Cocteau has just met Anna de Noailles, and I'm afraid he's already begun to talk like her—without stopping.

Matisse has returned from Morocco. He let me see his new paintings. They are truly remarkable. He has succeeded in making color an end in itself. But he doesn't seem to realize what he has achieved or, if he does, he is not content with it. It seems color is just one of the many problems he will address in his career as a painter. For the moment, he seems to have put it aside and is struggling with composition.

FEBRUARY 24, 1911

Apollinaire gave my paintings at the Devamez Gallery a perfunctory review in *L'Intransigeant*. Now I know how Rousseau must have felt. Of course, now that Rousseau is dead and the painters Apollinaire believes in won't back down about him, Apollinaire writes the unqualified reviews of Rousseau that would have made the poor man happy.

1911

The Irish sculptress Nuala O'Donel, who was a student of Rodin and a friend of Malvina Hoffman, purposely gassed herself yesterday in her studio. She's dead. Miss Hoffman is quite shaken by it. A rumor is circulating through the Hôtel Biron that Miss O'Donel was despondent because Rodin no longer came to see her work and didn't seem interested in it anymore.

I wish we could all stop caring what other people think of our work. Surely, we have a million examples, right here in the Hôtel Biron, of how dangerous this practice is.

1 9 1 1

Cocteau has managed to get himself hired by the Russian Ballet! He is painting publicity posters and writing advertisements for magazines. I knew he would insinuate himself into their company somehow.

I accompanied Rodin to the opening of the Société Nouvelle Salon at the Georges Petit Gallery. Rodin is its chairman, so he should not have been surprised by the work exhibited there. Nevertheless, he stood for a very long time in front of Jacques Blanche's portrait of the dancer Vaslav Nijinsky, as if he had never seen it before. I envy Rodin's capacity for awe.

Our show of Picasso watercolors at the 291 caused even more commotion than the Cézanne exhibit. But there have been some buyers, among them Arthur B. Davies, a painter who frequents the 291, and Stieglitz himself.

MAY 14, 1911

Rilke is back from North Africa, and he still has not written anything since *Malte Laurids Brigge*. He is seriously considering giving up writing altogether. Rodin, who never had a dry spell in his life until after he turned sixty, is trying to convince Rilke he has no right to quit, that it would be an arrogant rejection of his obligations in life to do so. Rilke was respectful to Rodin but in private said that Rodin is no example, that he has let his life become "grotesque and ridiculous." He wouldn't let Rodin's age or ill health serve as an excuse, as Matisse thought it should. Rilke still admires Rodin too much and as a result can only be disappointed by his humanness, his foibles, and the infirmities of his old age.

MAY 1911

The American Duchess claims that some street toughs broke into Rodin's rooms here at the Hôtel Biron a few nights ago, held him at gunpoint, and tried to steal some of his work, but she brandished her own pistol and frightened them off. No one believes her. Now people in the house are worried about Rodin's collection of revolvers. There seem to be quite a lot of them, which no one realized before. The Duchess has acquired a guard dog for Rodin, hired a detective, and sits up in an armchair while the master sleeps. She's driving everyone crazy.

SUMMER 1911

Picasso is summering in Céret in the Pyrénées. He is staying in an abandoned monastery surrounded by a wild garden, where he has taken all the rooms on the first floor. Sounds like Rodin here at the Hôtel Biron!

Braque, Max Jacob, and some other friends are visiting him. Matisse even plans to go down there. Picasso writes us that he likes the Catalan people, and that Max Jacob is earning extra pocket money by reading their horoscopes in the local café. The town butcher gave Picasso a red curtain he had admired, and Picasso has hung it in his studio.

JULY 1911

Yesterday Rodin presided over a meeting of the women's society called the Internationales to honor Valentine St. Point. A homage to Rodin was read at the meeting. Miss St. Point was blasted in the press this morning for her novels. *Le Cri de Paris* said the first one is about a woman achieving sexual satisfaction, the second about incest, the third self-gratification, and they ridiculed Rodin for admiring her, implying that he was duped by her novels' eroticism.

SEPTEMBER 21, 1911

The tenants of the Hôtel Biron are talking about a suggestion made by Apollinaire in *L'Intransigeant* that a warranty office be created for artwork, which would regulate and supervise payment of a percentage to artists when their work is resold at a higher value. Rilke thinks it is an idea before its time but hopes the system will eventually be employed. Picasso thinks it is a high-minded idea but impossible to execute, and that dealers would find some way to circumvent it. Matisse said that painters should think about creating art for its own sake and not try to become rich from it—that profit is the artist's downfall.

1 9 1 1

Max Jacob's novel *Saint Matorel* has been published with four etchings by Picasso. Kahnweiler, the gallery owner who sometimes shows Picasso's work, had it published.

Rodin has been complaining lately that he's thirsty all the time, so his doctor told him to drink milk instead of wine. The American Duchess is administering it to him. The tenants of the Hôtel Biron are grumbling that this doctor is a quack. The doctor doesn't pretend to know what's wrong with Rodin, only how to cure his thirstiness. We'll see. Picasso is also ill and has been advised by a different doctor to remove all spices from his diet.

Matisse has canceled his painting classes. He says he is not a teacher, only a painter. He says he tried to get his students to stop imitating his style and instead learn the fundamentals in order to find their own direction, but he failed. He seems discouraged and disheartened by the whole experience. The students are very disappointed that he has decided to quit and are trying to change his mind, but he won't be budged.

Rodin gave a lecture on cathedrals today to another ladies' group. He shocked them by going into raptures comparing the Gothic cathedral to a woman's body. He used some rather suggestive language. I always thought one could speak rather romantically in French and get away with it—in English any emotion always sounds more vulgar—but apparently I am wrong, because the ladies were shocked. Rodin was oblivious to having offended them.

DECEMBER 1911

Rodin is working on three different busts of Clemenceau, but the ex-prime minister won't sit for him as much as Rodin would like him to. Clemenceau doesn't like the busts; he says the first one looks Japanese.

JANUARY 1912

Rodin and the Duchess have gone to Rome to preside over the unveiling of *The Walking Man* in the courtyard of the Farnese Palace. The Duchess has also arranged for Rodin to meet with John Marshall, a representative of the Metropolitan Museum of Art in New York.

1912

Cocteau's third book of poems, *The Dance of Sophocles*, has been released. I'm afraid that André Gide has given it a bad review, implying that Cocteau thinks too much of himself. The talk around the Hotel Biron is that Gide is a Jansenist and Cocteau is not, and this difference prejudiced Gide's review.

Everyone seems to be taking the Cubism that Picasso and Braque started and running off with it in all directions. The Dutch and the Russians have developed something called Orphism, which attempts to arrive at pure abstraction in color and form. Picasso hates this; it doesn't include enough of the messy reality that is his raw material. Gris and Léger are working on a cylindrical form of Cubism (no irony intended). The Futurists in Italy and the Vorticists in Russia claim to have been inspired by Cubism. Picasso says Cézanne started everything, and Picasso, for his part, just tries to take art a step further whenever he can. He and Braque are working on high analytical Cubism now. I'm sure Picasso and Braque will take the work to its furthest point and then move on to something else the way Matisse does, while their followers spend the rest of their lives mulling over the ramifications of Cubism.

Satie's career is definitely relaunched. A few months ago Ravel played a few of Satie's works at the Société Indépendante Musicale, and Debussy played something called *Gymnopédies* at the Cercle Musical. Roland Manuel just performed the *Prélude de la Porte Héroique du Ciel* at SIM. Now the critics can't stop praising him.

Satie was pleased at first, but now he's annoyed because people only want to hear the work he wrote before he went into seclusion. He says those pieces are all twenty years old. He wants his new work to be performed.

FEBRUARY 1912

Rodin and the Duchess have returned from Rome. I'm afraid the Duchess made a nuisance of herself again. She insisted that *The Walking Man* be placed in the very center of the Farnese Palace courtyard, where it blocks traffic, and nowhere else. Camille Barrière, the French ambassador, did not want the figure in the courtyard at all and certainly not in the very center, where it would be an obstruction. But he gave in.

The Duchess' digestive problem was also aggravated by the trip. (She cannot keep any food down.) She had to leave the table repeatedly during meals when she was dining with the Marshalls. I imagine this made it very disturbing and unpleasant for them. The tenants of the Hôtel Biron have nicknamed the Duchess "The Infection" and want her out.

Rodin hadn't been to Rome in thirty years. He said he enjoyed sightseeing alone and being honored with banquets. He said everything is big there, the men expressive, the women natural. He wished they wouldn't dress in Parisian styles.

1912

Since the ballet *Schéhérazade* was such a hit, Diaghilev plans to stage another Oriental ballet and has asked Cocteau to write the libretto.

Picasso and Fernande have ended their association. Fernande said their life changed so much after Picasso became financially comfortable that she no longer knew how to be his companion. Picasso has taken up with a girl he calls Eva.

MAY 13, 1912

The premiere of Coctcau's ballet was a failure. Cocteau is wandering around the garden sulking, and various tenants of the Hôtel Biron are watching him from their windows, wondering what they should say, if anything, to console him. I imagine that if anyone understands what the public failure of a work of art feels like, it would be Rodin.

MAY 28, 1912

Everyone is in an uproar over Nijinsky's *Afternoon of a Faun.* Debussy did the music, and the libretto was drawn from Mallarmé's poem. Nijinsky was wearing a skintight leotard with faun spots on it, a little tail protruding from the back, and a cluster of grapes in front to serve as a fig leaf. He portrayed a faun haunted by nymphs who leave him a scarf to remember them by. Apparently, in an unrehearsed gesture, he lay down on the scarf and aped the sex act at the end. Rodin thought it was quite beautiful.

MAY 30, 1912

Rodin was so thrilled with Nijinsky's performance of *The Afternoon of a Faun* two nights ago that he went backstage afterward to congratulate the dancer. The next day, Rodin was willing to sign his name to a defense of that performance written by Roger Marx, which was then published in *Le Matin* as an answer to Calmette's article in *Le Figaro,* attacking Nijinsky's performance as filthy, bestial, and lecherous.

Calmette's answer to Rodin's article appeared in this morning's *Figaro.* He's a shrewd editor; I'm not surprised he has so much power. Instead of dwelling on Nijinsky's performance, he attacked Rodin, saying that he displays his lewd draw-

ings of women in the chapel here at the Hôtel Biron, and that
the French state has purchased the Hôtel so the taxpayer can
subsidize Rodin while he lives here, at a cut rate, desecrating
the place with his eroticism.

Rodin is going to retract his *Le Matin* article, but that will
only anger his friends and remind them of his refusal to sell
his *Balzac* to a group of pro-Dreyfusards fifteen years ago. His
enemies will add desecrator of churches to his other sins.

SUMMER 1912

Picasso took Eva to Céret for the summer, but Fernande was staying there with the Pichots, so Picasso and Eva
left for Avignon and ended up in Sorgues, a town just to the
north. Braque and his wife have joined them.

Nijinsky has been coming over to pose for Rodin. Today
Diaghilev caught them napping in Rodin's studio and flew into
a jealous rage. Cocteau was delighted. He says Rodin is the
only one who, by virtue of his position and power, could make
Diaghilev feel truly threatened, and he assured Rodin that
Mr. D. would never let Nijinsky return to pose. Rodin acted
wounded, claimed nothing unusual had occurred, and complained that he is not far along enough in his sculpture to do
without Nijinsky.

The tenants of the Hôtel Biron say Cocteau is looking at
Rodin in a new way now and has begun to wear lipstick for him.

AUGUST 1912

Picasso painted a picture on the wall of his rented villa
in Sorgues that he wants to preserve, so Kahnweiler is having
the wall removed and shipped to Paris. Picasso has also asked
Kahnweiler to move his belongings from his studio to another
in Montparnasse so he and Eva won't return to the studio
where he stayed with Fernande. However, he plans to keep his
room here at the Hôtel Biron.

SEPTEMBER 30, 1912

Stieglitz sent me the *New York Times* article on Rodin's break with the Duchess, which was published two weeks ago. They portrayed her as domineering and unreasonable, and Rodin as duped by her aristocratic title.

Rilke is complaining that Rodin is depressed because he doesn't sculpt anymore and doesn't know how to regain his dignity now that the Duchess has made a fool of him.

After much letter writing and desperate pleading, Cocteau has finally met Gide. Cocteau was hoping for a mentor and a good review of *The Dance of Sophocles,* but I'm afraid Gide was as petulant as ever and simply told Cocteau to change his handwriting. (Cocteau uses purple ink and employs a florid style copied from Anna de Noailles.) Cocteau is hurt, as could be expected.

OCTOBER 14, 1912

In a couple of articles that appeared this week, one in *Le Temps* and the other in *L'Intermédiare,* Apollinaire has attempted to explain Cubism to the public. I'm afraid he spends too much time defending it, defending his defense of it, and insisting that it is a French form of art. (Parisians won't like any form of art if they suspect it to be un-French, and Apollinaire, who is Polish, shares both this reasoning and this weakness.) But he does say something about the history of Cubism and what it attempts to do. This may help the public appreciate it more. I hope so.

MARCH 1913

To celebrate the closing of the Armory Show, the students at the Art Institute of Chicago have burned in effigy Matisse's *Blue Nude.*

After the vicious attacks on him by critics in *The New York Times,* Matisse takes this new development very hard. I believe he was hoping that at least the young art students in America would appreciate his work, but even they are outraged by it. It made me wonder if now he misses his own students, who appreciated his innovations and wanted to copy him. When I asked him, he conceded that he missed their sympathy but felt that he had made the right decision in closing the school because he had expended so much energy trying to understand what each student was trying to do in his painting. He said he couldn't be a teacher and a painter at the same time.

Rodin is putting his finishing touches on the Clemenceau bust. Clemenceau is complaining that he looks like a Mongol general. His wife doesn't like the bust and has advised Clemenceau not to accept it. Clemenceau tells everyone he doesn't like Rodin because the sculptor is vain, stupid, and cares too much about money. Rodin complains that Clemenceau is surly and condescending.

Rilke is back from trips to Austria, Spain, and Venice and is celebrating the demise of the American Duchess. Rilke quibbles with the reasons Rodin banished her from the Hôtel Biron (he is perpetually disappointed with Rodin's reasoning in the area of human relations) but is feeling too victorious about her dismissal to let that bother him.

Everyone in the Hôtel Biron is debating the truth of the rumor that, before she left, the American Duchess was poisoning Rodin's milk with arsenic. No one denies Rodin is ill, but there is considerable speculation about the cause.

END OF MARCH 1913

Miss Camille Claudel has been locked up in a lunatic asylum! Her own brother, the writer Paul Claudel, arranged it. In France, any family member can obtain a doctor's certificate authorizing internment, and that's enough to put you away for life. Only your family can get you out again. It's terrifying!

I knew Paul Claudel was a prig and disapproved of his sister's profession as a sculptress, her failure to marry, her affair with Rodin twenty-five long years ago. But I had no idea he would do anything like this. People in the house say that Miss Claudel's sister and mother also disapprove of her, and that it was only her father who kept them from doing this before. A week after her father dies, they lock her up!

Miss Claudel does act a bit odd at times, but certainly no more so than a hundred other artists in Paris, who are considered merely eccentric. She has harmed no one. She was working and is well-respected among other artists.

People in the house are waiting to see what Rodin is planning to do about this. Only some kind of public outcry could possibly get Miss Claudel released.

END OF MARCH 1913

Rodin has cleared all Camille's belongings out of the room he was letting her use, and he has offered it to Nijinsky!

MAY 1913

Cocteau has just witnessed the "scandal" at the opening of the Russian Ballet's *Rite of Spring*, and he's now suffering from the misconception that all great art is sprung from the desire to rebel. Several tenants of the Hôtel Biron would like to tell him otherwise, but Diaghilev has asked Cocteau to astound him, and right now Cocteau's primary motivation is to do just that.

1913

In a further effort to astound Diaghilev, Cocteau is trying to induce dreams. To do this, he eats several boxes of sugar, then stops his ears with wax and lies down. He does this twice a day. The rest of the household is awaiting the results with great trepidation.

JUNE 1913

Picasso has returned to Céret for the summer. He has written to Apollinaire saying that his father died, that Eva is ill, and that he has taken Max Jacob across the border to Spain to see the bullfights.

Rodin has returned from a trip to Knole to visit his friend Lady Sackville. She took him to a Louis XIV costume ball. He wants to do Lady S.'s bust and complains that she treats him like her father (she is fifty-one, he seventy-two). He also profited from the visit by choosing a site in the Victoria flower gardens for a copy of *The Burghers* to be installed.

FALL 1913

Cocteau has just returned from Normandy with the results of his sleep experiments. The book is called *The Potomak*. It's about a winged, gelatinous monster who lives in an aquarium under the Place de la Madeleine and eats gloves and spelling errors. In the book, Cocteau and his friends visit the monster. Cocteau claims the book started out as drawings, and its subject is really the moltings of intelligence as revealed by occult characters experiencing an entire range of deep confusions. Cocteau keeps insisting that this book is his first major breakthrough because, whereas before all his books were the product of consciousness, this one is the result of sleep. He says he owes it all to *The Rite of Spring* and has dedicated his new book to Stravinsky. His publisher for his poetry, the *Mercure de France*, has agreed to print it.

Nijinsky got married to one of the dancers in the Russian Ballet on their tour to South America. Diaghilev didn't go because he's afraid of traveling by boat. Cocteau says Mr. D. will be more upset by being replaced by a girl of twenty-three than by losing Nijinsky, and will find some way to dismiss him from the company. Today Nijinsky brought his new wife over to the Hôtel Biron to meet Rodin. Cocteau won't speak to Nijinsky anymore and stayed in the sacristy. I think Cocteau loves the intrigue of the Russian Ballet; it makes our house full of artists seem so tame by comparison.

NOVEMBER 1913

Apollinaire published reproductions of Picasso's Cubist constructions in his new magazine, *Les Soirées de Paris*. Now all his subscribers are canceling.

Matisse's *Portrait of a Woman* in this year's Salon d'Automne has received rave reviews from Apollinaire in *Les Soirées de Paris*. Apollinaire has knighted Matisse as the first Voluptuary since Renoir.

Rodin is working on a bust of Lady Sackville. He is fascinated with her long hair (down to her thighs) and has asked her to go to the Riviera with him this winter. Rodin invited the Count of Montesquiou over to watch the sittings, but complains that he talks too much about himself. Rodin has hired a man to serve them tea and cakes while wearing white gloves. I think he's the produce man!

DECEMBER 1913

There have finally been some articles in the Paris newspapers about Camille Claudel's incarceration in a lunatic asylum. But since October, Paul Claudel has been in Hamburg on a diplomatic assignment and won't respond to any of the accusations. People in the house have asked Rodin to do something, but he won't. I think he remembers the Nijinsky imbroglio last year and the Dreyfus affair many years ago, and refuses to take any public stand on any issue that might draw personal attacks on him.

Rilke is outraged and thinks it is the most selfish thing Rodin has ever done. Other people in the Hôtel Biron think Rodin might prefer to have Camille out of Paris because he seems to feel victimized by the women who love him and to wish they would go away. But he does not seem to have the will to send them away himself, as with Rose or the Duchess.

I wish there were some way to get Miss Claudel out of that asylum. It frightens me to think this can happen. Cocteau says Gwen John was acting awfully peculiar when Rodin stopped

seeing her, but no one locked her up. Rilke explained that
away by saying she is English, and the English have a way of
letting all their emotions out at once and acting totally wild for
a few weeks. Then they return to normal as if nothing at all had
happened. Rilke always attributes behavior to nationality or
"race," as he calls it. Picasso says the difference between Camille Claudel and Gwen John is that Gwen John's brother
chose to comfort her instead of lock her up, and Picasso would
never do such a thing to a sister no matter how strange or
embarrassing her behavior. Cocteau said Camille and Rodin
ended their affair twenty years ago, and it is romanticism to
attribute her demise to that; but others in the house, including
Rilke, said that her brother Paul still blames Rodin for ruining
her reputation and steering her toward a career in sculpture
(even though she had already established it as her profession
before she met Rodin). It is her brother who makes the connection, not us.

DECEMBER 3, 1913

As expected, Diaghilev has dismissed Nijinsky from
the Russian Ballet. Everyone is furious. Nijinsky is taking it
very hard. Massine has become Mr. D.'s new companion.

JANUARY 1914

Apollinaire has nicknamed Picasso "The Bird of Be-
nin" after some bronze bird with a butterfly in its beak that
originates from there.

Apollinaire has used the Autumn Salon in Berlin last fall
and an article in *Les Soirées de Paris* this month to glorify Rousseau. I like the publicity it gives Rousseau's work, but I am
suspicious of Apollinaire's motives. Apollinaire is so excessive
in his praise, it's as if he was embarrassed that he was lukewarm
about Rousseau at first, and now he's either trying to make us
forget his error or to make amends for it. Either way, it makes
me uncomfortable.

I'm also disturbed by the way Apollinaire insists on per-

LAURA MARELLO

petuating myths about Rousseau. He says his work was discovered, when it was not. He says his work was encouraged, when it was not. He loves to retell only those anecdotes that make Rousseau seem quaint and naïve, like his arrest and his belief in ghosts. Why do critics insist on making myths out of artists? Why can't artists just be people who happen to paint or sculpt or compose music and also happen to possess a cross section of the oddities of human nature, just like other regular people?

Vincent Van Gogh's letters have just been published in Paris, and people in the Hôtel Biron are reading them. Rilke was quick to point out that when Van Gogh lost his mind for brief periods, it was his own choice to seek help in an asylum; then, he knew he could get out whenever he felt ready. Camille Claudel's doctors have said she is well, but she still cannot be released without her family's consent, which they will not give. Matisse pointed out that Van Gogh had commited violence against himself and others and still had a choice, whereas Camille has not hurt anyone and was locked up against her will. Picasso reiterated his brother theme—Van Gogh had a brother who tried to help him, whereas Camille's brother seems out to destroy her.

Cocteau was struck by the fact that when Van Gogh was doing what is considered to be his best work, he considered himself a failure. This sparked a discussion about the possibilities of judging your own work, and the necessity to keep on working when you don't know if it's good or not.

We eventually got back to talking about Miss Claudel. No one knows what to do. If the doctors in the asylum can't get her released and the uproar in the press doesn't produce results, we are all at a loss to know what to do. Her family says she has a persecution complex. My goodness, wouldn't *anyone* who was locked up against his will and against the advice of his doctors?

I do hear that someone managed to smuggle her papers and artwork out of her Quai Bourbon studio before her family destroyed everything. Her sons visit her daily in the asylum and are smuggling in supplies so she can work at night in secret. (She is forbidden to do her artwork in the asylum!) Her dealer, Eugène Blot, is planning an exhibit in hopes this might force her release.

FEBRUARY 1914

Nijinsky has a contract with the Palace Theatre in London for the spring season. He and his sister are rehearsing here in Paris, but no one thinks he will be able to make it without Diaghilev. Mr. D. is making as much trouble for Nijinsky as he can. He has taken legal action to prevent Nijinsky's sister from dancing with him on the grounds that her resignation was not accepted by his Russian Ballet. Nijinsky is a nervous wreck, and some people are afraid he might snap.

MARCH 1914

When Cocteau can't satisfy his need for intrigue by observing the clashes within the Russian Ballet, he inevitably ends up creating his own. Cocteau ran off to Switzerland a few weeks ago to convince Stravinsky to write the music for his new ballet *David*. Of course, Diaghilev found out, and he's furious because he thinks Cocteau is trying to take Stravinsky away from his work on *The Nightingale*, which Diaghilev already commissioned. Stravinsky patched it up with Diaghilev by promising to finish *The Nightingale* before beginning work on *David*. In the meantime, Cocteau wants to go back to Switzerland to work with Stravinsky, but he keeps making dates and canceling because he is afraid of the epidemic of scarlet fever there. When he does finally insist on going, it's usually because Stravinsky has wired him not to come—either because he hasn't finished *The Nightingale,* or because his wife is too sick, or because he's off to Berlin on business. I'm sure Cocteau is driving him crazy.

Max Jacob has just published a book of poems called *The Siege of Jerusalem*, with illustrations by Picasso (three etchings and drypoints) and published by Kahnweiler.

MARCH 1914

Nijinsky came down with influenza and was unable to fulfill his contract at the Palace Theatre in London. He is trying to persuade Diaghilev to pay him his back salary from the Russian Ballet, but apparently nothing was ever written down. Mr. D. paid Nijinsky's food and hotel bills, and reinvested the remainder of Nijinsky's salary in the ballet company. Nijinsky also earned enormous sums, which he never actually received, to dance at private parties.

APRIL 1914

Rodin has returned from three months on the Riviera. His book *The Cathedrals of France* has just been published, but as usual Rodin cannot enjoy an untarnished success. The Paris Municipal Council passed a resolution that prohibits municipal libraries from purchasing the book. A rumor is circulating that the text was not written by Rodin, as is the criticism that the drawings are rudimentary and beneath a schoolchild. Several prominent Paris writers believe the book is a hoax. Reviews are appearing that cite numerous errors of fact and claim that Rodin doesn't know anything about cathedrals. Some people think his critics are just angry that he has not used the book to take a stand about the church-state battle. But they should not be surprised, since Rodin has always avoided political issues.

Cocteau finally went to Switzerland when he was least welcome and has just come back. The word around the Hôtel Biron is that the meeting was a disaster, even though Cocteau pretends it wasn't. Apparently, Stravinsky is not really that interested in *David* and is still trying to finish *The Nightingale*, and Cocteau behaved badly. I think Stravinsky is embarrassed by Cocteau's slavish adoration and by his persistence.

MAY 1914

Charles Morice, the Symbolist poet and editor of Rodin's *Cathedrals of France*, gave a reading from the new book today at the Hôtel Biron. Rodin seemed to enjoy it most and acted as if he had never heard it before.

Nijinsky is well again and has vowed to keep dancing but to hire someone else to administer his company. He went to the premiere of the Russian Ballet's season at the Opera, but everyone was cold to him, including Cocteau. People say the Russian Ballet has no magic now that Nijinsky has been thrown out. I agree.

JUNE 23, 1914

Picasso is hopping mad. His friend Apollinaire just published an article in *The Paris Journal* that says all the Montmartre painters have moved to Montparnasse, where they get high on cocaine, wear American clothes, and frequent cafés. He even lists which painters frequent which cafés!

Nijinsky and his wife had a baby girl and named her Kyra. Diaghilev invited Nijinsky back to the Russian Ballet, but only to save the company, which no one likes anymore without Nijinsky. Nijinsky tried to go back, but everyone was so cold to him that it broke his heart and he has quit again.

1914

Cocteau is sulking over his break (as he calls it) with Stravinsky and insists that despite the failure of *David* and Stravinsky's indifference to him, he will cherish their time together in Switzerland the way Nietzsche cherished his time with Wagner at Tribschen. In private, Stravinsky says this is all rubbish and that he was never close to Cocteau in the first place, so there can have been no break.

Maurice Rostand has "broken" with Cocteau because Rostand discovered that Proust had been friends with Cocteau all along, and Cocteau didn't tell Maurice or introduce him, even though Proust had seen Maurice at the Opera and requested Cocteau to introduce them.

People in the Hôtel Biron have been speculating on why Cocteau hasn't tried to exploit his friendship with Proust the way he has with Diaghilev and Stravinsky. The consensus of opinion seems to be that it's because Proust is a stay-at-home and not in the public eye, so there's no opportunity for exploitation. It has also been ventured that Proust is too much like Cocteau, frail and vicious.

When Cocteau gets older, I wonder if he will draw young men of talent into his circle and treat them as he wished to be treated by Diaghilev and Stravinsky, or if he will punish them by rejecting them in order to get even for the humiliation he suffered, fawning over great men who neglected him. Maybe both. Or perhaps he'll play the young boys off against each other for sport. I'm afraid he has a malicious streak.

MID-JULY 1914

Cocteau has met some of the other Cubists, and people in his circle feel threatened, because he can't mix socially with his aristocratic friends and with the Cubists at the same time. Rodin had dinner at the American Embassy with Theodore Roosevelt, Henri Bergson, Edith Wharton, and Cornelius Vanderbilt.

AUGUST 2, 1914

French soldiers have confiscated Rodin's car, his horse, and his workmen, and advised him not to ship any sculptures to London. They've given him forty-eight hours to move all his artwork into the cellar.

SEPTEMBER 1914

Cocteau has organized a convoy of ambulances and left for the front lines. Rodin and Rose went to London with Judith Cladel, but people in the house say they've heard reports that he is not happy there.

Picasso and Eva have returned to Paris after their summer in Avignon. Picasso is very irritated by the war. He said when he saw Braque and Derain off at the railway station in Avignon last month he was afraid he'd never see them again. Kahnweiler has fled, we assume to a neutral country. Apollinaire applied for French nationality, and when he received it, joined the artillery. Picasso is calling the war a gross stupidity.

NOVEMBER 1914

Rodin and Rose have moved to Rome, where Rodin is drawing from the model in an ice cream parlor (!!!) during its off-hours. Apparently, the parlor is a large rotunda with columns and marble tables, which he likes very much. But otherwise he is bored from lack of social opportunities, and people say he's sulking because no one pays attention to him anymore now that the war has begun.

Diaghilev has asked Nijinsky to dance with the Russian Ballet in New York, but Nijinsky's citizenship bars him from leaving Europe during the war.

Stieglitz wrote me that *Camera Work* is going to fold, and he won't be able to use our articles right now. He did say, though, that he plans to start another magazine sometime in the near future and hopes we won't give the articles to another publisher. The tenants of the Hôtel Biron say they have no intention of giving away their manuscripts. Picasso, Matisse, Satie, and Nijinsky aren't finished with theirs and plan to continue working on them. So do I. Rilke suggested I write to Miss Claudel with the news and ask her to hold on to her manuscript for possible future publication by Stieglitz.

DECEMBER 1914

Cocteau is back from ambulance duty on the front lines. He is trying to get Maurice Barrès to publish an article in *L'Echo de Paris* about the bombing of Rheims. He feels that too much has been said about the cathedral and not enough about the human suffering.

Max Jacob has converted to Christianity and been baptized. He asked Picasso to be his godfather. Picasso agreed.

APRIL 1915

Rodin has returned to Rome to do a bust of the Pope. I hear he is unhappy, though, because the Pope only granted him three sittings when he had requested twelve, and the Pope would not let him look down at the top or at the back or sides of his head.

Nijinsky was given permission to go to America to dance for Diaghilev, but they are already fighting. Nijinsky wants Mr D. to pay him his back salary before he agrees to dance.

FALL 1915

Rodin has returned from Rome but complains of the cold. Coal is in short supply.

Cocteau continues to publish his magazine, *Le Mot.* He wants to stage *A Midsummer Night's Dream* at the Cirque Médrano and to use music from Satie's *Gymnopédies.*

Matisse has been back from his summer home in Nice for several months now. In America, only the rich summer in the country and winter in the city; but here all the painters do it, and they are not rich. I suppose it also seems odd during wartime, when all rituals of behavior have been suspended; but the painters in Paris, including the tenants of the Hôtel Biron, travel even more than they did before the war.

I had the opportunity to go down to Matisse's studio and take a look at his new work. I don't know what to make of it. All the pictures are done in different styles, composed in dif-

ferent manners, use color and brushstrokes differently. I am
not sure what Matisse is after, and I am not sure whether this
variety is a search for something in particular or a symptom of
the disruption of the war. In either case, Matisse is furiously
at work; he knows he is after something, but he does not know
what it is. The most curious feature of his new work, and the
only thing I can see common to this wildly variant work, is his
use of erasure. Matisse scratches out certain forms on a canvas
but leaves their traces visible. Someday this technique will be
the rage in New York. I must tell Alfred Stieglitz about it.
There is something fussy and irritable about it that would
appeal to a New York painter.

DECEMBER 1915

Picasso's companion, Eva, has died. He is taking it
very hard.

Cocteau is in raptures. He has fallen in love with Picasso.
He says the experience was one of the major revelations of his
life, on a par with seeing Stravinsky's *Rite of Spring*. He has
focused all his admiration on Picasso now. A few days ago, he
visited the painter, wearing a harlequin costume concealed
under a trenchcoat. But Picasso seemed to like the idea and
even kept the costume. Picasso may be the first great man who
is generous enough to let Cocteau adore him.

Cocteau would like to collaborate on a ballet with Picasso.
This has made him realize that Diaghilev does not know about
modern art, and that the painters from Montmartre never go
to the Russian Ballet. From this he's beginning to understand
that there really is an artistic right and an artistic left in Paris,
and that no one has successfully aligned himself with both.
That's what his aristocratic friends were arguing about so
vehemently when he made friends with the other Cubists.

JANUARY 1916

Some charcoal drawings by a woman named Georgia O'Keeffe arrived by mail at the 291 a few weeks ago, and the photographs Stieglitz made to show them to me just reached me here in Paris. His note says the photos do not do justice to the drawings, but I think they would be the most amazing things I have ever seen, if I could actually see them. The drawings are abstract and convey with astonishing power and forthrightness what it must feel like to be a woman. Stieglitz wants to give this Georgia O'Keeffe a show.

Matisse brought me down to his studio to see the culmination of his experiments of the past year. The painting is called *The Piano Lesson.* It takes elements from Cubism, Orphism, and abstraction and integrates them. The result is beyond categorization, except to say that it is a Matisse. His remarkable use of color is also in evidence. There's a feeling of foreboding in this painting that I have never seen before in a Matisse and may never see again, judging from his newer work. He is now doing paintings of models lounging in his studio, and he seems quite content with them. But we both know this satisfaction is only temporary. Matisse is like an advancing army. He is regrouping, gathering his forces. The next campaign will be launched soon.

Picasso is sketching portraits of Max Jacob and of Apollinaire with his head bandaged in his hospital room.

APRIL 1916

Cocteau is trying to convince Satie to collaborate with him on a ballet called *Parade.* He's taken voluminous notes and left them with Satie. He's also been posing for Picasso. I believe he still entertains the idea of Picasso also collaborating on the ballet. Picasso is trying to get Cocteau to go to the Italian hospital here to visit Apollinaire, who is suffering from a head wound he got in the trenches. Cocteau likes Picasso's instinct for trying to bring people together, but Cocteau says he's heard that Apollinaire doesn't like him, and he doesn't think it would be appropriate to go to visit him. Picasso has also been introducing Cocteau to other painters, among them Modigliani and Max Jacob. Cocteau seems to like that, but says everyone except Picasso is suspicious of him because of his Russian Ballet associations.

Picasso gave up his studio in Montparnasse to take a house in the suburb of Montrouge. Since Satie still has an apartment nearby in Arceuil, they often walk home together in the middle of the night. Transportation is impossible with this war on.

MAY 1916

Nijinsky was a big success in America, but Diaghilev and the Russian Ballet have left for Spain without him. He and Mr. D. fought the entire time, and Diaghilev does not want him to dance for the company anymore, even if it ruins them. Nijinsky's wife says that Diaghilev is trying to ruin Nijinsky. I'm afraid this is quite possible.

AUGUST 1916

Rodin had another stroke and fell down the stairs at the Villa des Brillants in Meudon.

Picasso has agreed to do *Parade* with Cocteau and Satie. Cocteau is thrilled. He feels that Picasso painting for the Russian Ballet will be the scandal he's longing to create, the collaboration of the artistic left and right that everyone claimed was impossible.

SEPTEMBER 1916

Cocteau is sulking about *Parade*. Apparently, Picasso and Satie enjoy working together so much that Cocteau feels left out. The talk around the Hôtel Biron seems to confirm this. Satie seems to like Picasso's ideas about the libretto better than Cocteau's. Third parties are trying to get Picasso to assuage Cocteau's hurt feelings.

SEPTEMBER 1916

Picasso talked to Cocteau and convinced him that all three of them see eye to eye, and that Satie is simply confused by the different approaches of Cocteau and Picasso. Cocteau has agreed to allow Picasso to clear things up with Satie. The situation has reached that point where it's impossible to tell who is lying to whom; but Cocteau appreciates Picasso's gesture to placate him, and I'm sure he appreciates the intrigue, even though in this case he would not admit it.

OCTOBER 1916

Diaghilev agreed to send some of his dancers back to New York to dance with Nijinsky, but he did not send them back in time for adequate rehearsals. Nijinsky's nerves are a wreck from trying to manage, choreograph, and direct the company—something he vowed never to attempt again. The dancers are giving him trouble—they even organized a two-day strike—and some people believe Diaghilev asked them to cause Nijinsky grief and to sabotage his work. Considering Diaghilev's malicious streak, this is altogether possible.

DECEMBER 1916

The senate passed a law making the Hôtel Biron into a Rodin museum and accepting all of Rodin's works as gifts to the French state. There was still a lot of objection to it; the senators called him demented, and his work dangerous and offensive. The erotic drawings in the chapel were discussed again. But the law finally passed, and Rodin has not heard about the charges against him. I hope they will not evict us until the war is over.

A banquet was held in honor of Apollinaire. Cocteau and Picasso attended. A fight broke out between the Cubists and Dadaists. When the banquet ended, Cocteau went to Diaghilev's New Year's Eve party, where he argued with a Cubist.

JANUARY 1917

Parade is scheduled to debut in May. Diaghilev is buying Cubist paintings. Mr. D. wants to rehearse *Parade* in Rome, but Satie doesn't want to go.

Rodin married Rose so if he dies first, she will have some financial protection. I don't think he even knows what is going on—Judith Cladel arranged it.

Cocteau and Picasso have left for Rome to work on *Parade*. Satie stayed behind.

FEBRUARY 14, 1917

Rose died in her sleep early this morning.

MAY 18, 1917

Parade premiered this afternoon at the Théâtre du Châtelet. The crowd was probably more mixed than it has ever been for a Paris premiere of the Russian Ballet. Diaghilev's society people were there, a notable group of counts and princesses. But the Montmartre and Montparnasse painters showed up for the first time (Diaghilev sent them free tickets), and there was a large contingent of Russian soldiers on leave.

The audience liked Picasso's drop curtain—a very sweet depiction of a winged horse, a harlequin, and some circus people sitting around backstage. But when the curtain rose and Satie's music started, everyone went crazy. It sounded like a circus. A few of the dancers were dressed up in these Cubist towers. The dancers jumped up and down and tripped over themselves.

Of course, the counts and princesses booed, the painters shouted, Vive Picasso! Vive Satie! from the upper balconies, and the soldiers joined in the bedlam. People said the ballet was "un-French" and inappropriately gleeful during wartime. Fistfights erupted, and people shouted death threats against Diaghilev, Picasso, and Satie. Women brandished their hatpins. Throughout the spectacle, Satie sat in the first row of the balcony, applauding madly.

JUNE 1917

Young composers have been flocking to Satie since the scandal of *Parade* has made him esteemed in the art world. Today Satie's protégés gave a concert here at the Hôtel Biron. It was organized by Blaise Cendrars. Satie calls his troupe The New Young Ones and plans to organize a public concert for them at the Vieux Columbier Theater.

But Satie is no longer following the line of thinking he set up for his protégés when he composed *Parade*. He has gone completely in the opposite direction. He's working on very sober music, which he deems appropriate to Plato's *Dialogues*.

Nijinsky is in Spain working with Diaghilev. They seem to be getting along, but Nijinsky has become a Tolstoy fanatic (concerning himself with peasant farming, vegetarianism, asceticism), and his wife is afraid Diaghilev is using the Tolstoyans to break up their marriage. As a result, she doesn't want Nijinsky to go to South America with Diaghilev.

JULY 1917

Nijinsky refused to go to South America with Diaghilev, so Mr. D. had him arrested in Spain for breach of contract and forced him to go to South America against his will. Nijinsky's wife still maintains that Diaghilev and the Tolstoyans are trying to ruin their marriage. Picasso, who is still close to the ballet because of his new companion, Olga, says that Diaghilev is not in league with the Tolstoyans, and Nijinsky could have gone to South America willingly without fear of further entanglement with them. Picasso did admit, though, that Diaghilev probably does have plans to break up Nijinsky's marriage, more out of spite than out of love.

Picasso is worried that Nijinsky has become a little too fanatic about this Tolstoyan philosophy. Without the possibility of working harmoniously with Diaghilev, Picasso is afraid that the strain might be too much for Nijinsky and that he might lose his reason. What a choice—a family and insanity, or losing your family and working with that viper Diaghilev!

AUGUST 1917

Nijinsky is dancing in Rio and Buenos Aires with the Russian Ballet, but once again everyone in the company is doing their best to sabotage his work. He keeps having "accidents" and hurting himself. It's really frightening. He's stepped on a rusty nail on stage, had to avoid a falling iron beam, and in *Petrouchka* fell from the puppet's booth, which was not properly secured. Nijinsky's wife suspects foul play and has hired a detective.

Picasso has returned to Paris with Olga, who has left the Russian Ballet.

NOVEMBER 14, 1917

Rodin's 77th birthday. He has pneumonia, and no one thinks he will pull through. It's a pity he has to die because there is not enough coal, but a lot of people are dying in much more horrifying ways because of this war.

NOVEMBER 18, 1917

Rodin died this morning. His last words were in praise of Puvis de Chavannes. He also mentioned his "wife in Paris who needs money," so most people assume he was referring to Camille, but he could have been speaking philosophically about the Duchess.

I am not going to deliver an elegy here; nothing I could write would be adequate.

More backlash from the *Parade* scandal: Jean Poueigh is suing Satie for a lewd postcard Satie sent him as an answer to Poueigh's vicious attack on Satie in his review of *Parade* in *Le Temps*. Satie lost his appeal today and Cocteau, who appeared as a defense witness, was fined for threatening Poueigh's lawyer. Satie has been fined a thousand francs and must serve a week in prison.

The Russian Ballet has returned to Spain without Nijinsky, who is no longer under obligation to them. Picasso is afraid Nijinsky will never dance again and is afraid for his health, which seems to be failing from trying so hard to live both with and without Diaghilev.

1 9 1 7

The tenants of the Hôtel Biron have been listening to Satie work on his new music and, of course, everyone is talking about it. No one can even agree on what it is. Picasso says it's humorous, but Matisse insists it is only humorous on paper by virtue of the titles, directions, and marginal notes. Cocteau brought out his copy of *Sports and Divertissements* to prove his point. Cocteau insists that *Sports and Divertissements* is the supreme collaborative effort of calligraphy, painting, poetry, and music, and wishes he could do something comparable in his lifetime. Matisse tried to explain to the rest of us Satie's economy and the individuality in his keyboard style, his use of dissonance and spare two-part counterpoint, his appoggiaturas and sonorities built up on fourths; but none of us knows enough about music to understand him. Picasso insisted on the humor again, saying that the textual comments only mirror the irony and whimsy in the music itself. Nijinsky said he thought that if Rodin were still alive, he would like Satie's new music, but Rilke balked at the idea and said that if Rodin couldn't understand Wagner or Debussy, he certainly wouldn't have understood Satie. When Cocteau suggested that you can like art without understanding it, Rilke conceded that though this was true in principle, Rodin still would not have liked it.

I have joined the U.S. Signal Corps Photographic Section under Major Barnes. Barnes is returning to New York to run the School of Aerial Photography, so I will be in charge of operations here in Paris.

JANUARY 1918

Satie is once again despondent over his friend and nemesis, Debussy. He was very hurt last year when Debussy never sent him any word congratulating him on *Parade*. He finally sent Debussy what appears to have been a very nasty, retaliatory letter. Now, of course, Satie regrets it.

The other tenants of the Hôtel Biron say that Satie is not simply angry about *Parade* but about his entire friendship with Debussy. Satie has always been the broke one, the unrecognized one; and now that his work is acknowledged, it still remains on the fringes, unaccepted. Though he would not choose to compose any other music than what he has created, he still resents his position, and Debussy, of course, is his hair shirt, the constant reminder of the position that Satie himself had wanted to be in.

But Debussy is very sick and may even be dying, so Satie, of course, feels terrible that he caused Debussy any unpleasantness. What a tortured friendship that must be.

Picasso continues to be afraid that Nijinsky is losing his mind. Nijinsky flies into rages at his wife, walks headlong into traffic on the streets, draws pictures of red and black eyes, and sometimes wanders the streets carrying a cross. Nijinsky and his wife are leaving for Budapest to get help.

Picasso says he has never seen so many examples of human destruction as the result of lost or thwarted love as have passed through the Hôtel Biron: Camille Claudel, Rose, the Duchess, Gwen John, Nuala O'Donel, and now Nijinsky. He says that some things, like work, may be more important than love, but nothing is more painful—not death, not illness, not even the failure of work. Of course, he blames it on women. Rilke agreed with him up to that point. Rilke, our resident supporter of women's rights, blames it on men. They got into an enormous argument over it, neither one of them would back down, and gross generalizations about the differences between the sexes were flying all over the house.

JANUARY 1918

Picasso has taken a studio on the Right Bank on a street full of art dealers. His new dealer, Paul Rosenberg (Leonce's brother), has opened a gallery nearby. Paul Guillaume, who held a joint Picasso-Matisse exhibit, has his gallery in the Faubourg St-Honoré. Picasso's continued success seems assured.

APRIL 1918

I've returned exhausted from the Meuse-Argonne offensive, where we worked day and night out of a brewery building to produce French intelligence photos by the time they were needed.

SUMMER 1918

Apollinaire has married. Everyone hopes his health will improve. Picasso is summering in Biarritz, drawing portraits of the Rosenbergs, and painting murals with Apollinaire's verse on them. Picasso married Olga in a civil ceremony with Apollinaire, Max Jacob, and Cocteau as witnesses. He has promised her a Russian Orthodox ceremony.

LATE FALL 1918

Apollinaire has died. Picasso is so overcome that he has asked Cocteau to send out the notices to newspapers.

We received our eviction notice. We have a month to vacate. Everyone is making plans. Matisse has decided to move to the South of France permanently, most likely to Nice. Picasso and Olga plan to winter in Paris in their new apartment on the Right Bank, and to summer on the Riviera. Rilke is leaving for Munich right away; he doesn't even plan to ship his possessions. He says we can have what we want, and the French government can dispose of the rest. In honor of the Armistice, I have burned all my canvases in a big bonfire and have resolved to give up painting entirely. I plan to concentrate on photography, which I feel I'm better at. I am going to Voulangis for a time, and when I've recovered from the war, I plan to return to Paris and eventually to New York.

Stieglitz has written me that he would like to recommission our articles. He is starting a new magazine called *MSS* and would like to publish the articles in it. But I'm afraid we cannot find the manuscripts. Rodin was reading them shortly before his last illness, and Rilke suspects they were locked in the basement with his other possessions, which are now the property of the French state. We've discussed asking the government for them, but Picasso is afraid they would claim them as their property and suppress them. Matisse suggested we wait until we might be able to retrieve them safely. Everyone has agreed to do that. I have written to Miss Claudel, who has her manuscript in her possession, to tell her of the situation. Since Satie, Nijinsky, and I were not finished with our manuscripts when we gave them to Rodin to read, but continued to work on them, we too have at least a certain portion of our manuscripts in our keeping. **Q**

Hey to All My Family

In there, it was night, and cars passing outside, a long way off, and I saw the headlights inside, saw them rushing around the curves in roads, rushing past trees and under the leaves on branches. In there, the halls were long and shiny, and sounds echoed for a long time, echoed somewhere in the pipes, or in the ceiling, a thrum in a wall, in a vent, and then it whirred, but was it inside or outside my ear? I lay in bed there, and tried to detect, tried to know, tried to determine which side of the building, the pipe, the wall, the ear, it had come from—a light, a noise, a thought.

They brought me there, and locked the door, and the clock behind the cage on the wall didn't keep any time at all.

"There are things," they said.

I stayed where I was, at the base of the wall.

There was a thin mat on the floor where I was.

The room was white, and there was just the one window, and the mesh was doubled, had two layers, and was painted white.

"There are things," they said.

"What's he doing?" they whispered.

"Where is he?" they whispered.

I stayed at the wall.

A man said, "You're just a boy."

But I didn't know.

This was all near Boston.

Hey, I almost said.

Hey, I almost said.

Hey, Jesus.

Hey, Mom and Dad. Hey to Bobby and Helen. Hey, Cyril and Joe.

Hey to all my family. **Q**

Ox

So the train ride down. Slyo, Blokes, Varn, Neel, Sir, Hels, Helding, Harm, Bonelawn, and Starvation Peak. Bolts, flaps, lorns, tanks, steens, bears, knife-ties—the slag on the roadbed, a boy in a berth. Passing: bullrings, the gate route, the buttress, the light. The platform has a pump, a fellow selling food, a priest next to a post. In history: Men would shoot game from the moving windows. Grasshoppers would cover the track. The family had top East and family ancestors. The root in the caboose was the crummy. A cripple was bad. In the berth: The curtain blows. All right. You can see behind me how the house goes. He holds my hand. The berts, spinks, spears—and you bark your shin! Troutville has mountains named for the suffering of the settlers. Nosaje has mines and the largest graveyard in America. All the kinsmen were killed by Red Indians. Or all the children had the croup. (Or a train got stuck in the mud under the water.) We eat: river-snap stringbeans. Geet-rind sweet asparagus. Mint-jar olive-snipe. Stuffed duck. A chop. The other man there is a sailor. We pass: the lady in the lambhouse, for example. The girl in the curled-up thicket. Docks next to the wrecks. Birds: That is a Big-Boned Rover, found normally in warmer climes. This is an Open-Collared Marbink. A few lose their wings at one hundred feet—and sink. Inside the train there is a blue suitcase, a blue valise, a blue hatbox. There are letters and numbers on a wooden trunk. In the berth there are other blue things. They cross at the bottom, thin ones and the one that is thick. Everything is dark. A train is a safe place. On the train a fellow sells fruit and bread. The eyeskin is pinched and squinted on the rip. A lady waits at a door. (Father helps her through.) This is the view from the caboose. The highball means everything is all right. In history: The caboose comes loose. The first locomotive was built in a hollow in England. The man used this pig-iron. People said the first locomotive looked like his mother's body! This part was the feather and this part was the hat. This is the way into the city. At the outskirts her skirts come up, the buckles, the post. He runs to the rail. He swings his arms largely. He waves his hat. We lean over. There is a way to fall down and die in a doorway, you see. Armstrong, Happy Valley, Stink River, Almighty. Almighty: I do not know. Passing: Track. The animals run on the river sand, one by one. Skulls on the sidings are the real thing. This is the street with the house that looked like ours. This is a knot of the sort in the West, on the dog or on the ox slipping on the ice, all that weight tied on. The head is wet. The hooves come through the roof. There were sticks on the railroad—and a pick. This is the great and giant train: boxcar, flatcar, hopper, gondola, stock, caboose. Gravel, grain, rock, cinder, bulb, frog. The boy, the boy, the boy I wish I knew the names of the places. The hole in the berth, the curtain. We come through the thicket fast. There he is! He puts up the box, he pulls down along the silver rim. He holds his hand. He breathes.

And so the train glides into Chicago, on the sidings and the break. Oh, the train ride into Chicago, the hose, the high-ball, the backs, the lot. We went down. We held the rail. We held the porter's hand. There was a cart at the station—next to a yellow train in the snow. There were boys running on the track falling off for who falls off first. They sold food at a stand, and hats. Father walked. Mother said the niggers. The boy dropped all the bags. Was it the oak stick that got stuck and kept? Was it the cut in the cheek and the green? Did he see the one broken-open contour on the handle of the door? No. (But Father did.) The boy dropped on himself half the bags. Through the broken part in the fence the boy in the yards lost a ball through the broken part in his arms and the ball rolled through the broken part in the fence to you. We went: across the platform, across the track, off the roadbed, along the bank, along the rail, along the aisle, up the stair.

Into the berth. We roll so slowly out of Chicago, over the sidings, over the snow, and the cracked black break. In history: A train could be brought in dead. In history: They would hang men from the caboose. The porter would pull the curtain. The porter is coming closer. He keeps the stick straight and clean. He touches a spot on the wall. Everything is quiet. You can see the vase, the bottle, the bucket. You can see next to her how he stands and the way the town falls down. Here is the rip. The curtain is balled at the bottom and turned back, bunched under a ring. There is a sound over a boy in Virginia. We eat: peas, carrots, cream. Green-sleeve heart-beans. Three potatoes: boiled white, baked white, and the red marshmallowed sweet. He eats succotash. She eats black marrow. One cucumber sliced long. The cut-cut of meat. She says we are eating off spoons that a cardinal once used. The other man's father died the day he came home from the war. We pass a train passing. (A truck-train passes us.) The rocks got this color from the blood of an animal. On the fifteenth day of July 1881 said Confederates stop a train. The colonel shoots you blindfolded, through his legs, around his back. Certain settlers used the bones of their children to build houses. The sleepy conductor waves to the sleepy people. In the berth: You watch the sot on the window drop—water, or mud, or breath. You make the zag under the tower's churt, the bar of the gang-brush, the bell-circle and the birch, her cheek, her teeth, her tongue. Mother loves me! The porter holds the bolt. He breaks the bed down. He sets the sheets. We pass: Elephant Battle, Fort Bliss, Big Hatchet Park. The hank of a broken boat in the wood. The nearest, largest barn. A house with the top chopped off. He stands next to me. He turns back the blanket. He pulls the sheet that you can see the white. He pulls in the placket sleeve. There is the little bend, and then—I do not know! How old is your father? The family sleeps through the night. We eat: chunks of hot bread. A ham with a hole inside. An orange on a plate. There is a brown cut left and this melon, wet leaves, some berries, and fat. The butter is bad. A glass falls on the floor. In history: There was a dead man for breakfast every morning. In a wooden trunk on the train there are coats, dresses, scarves, and a blue suit and shoes. She says these men will eat me from the feet up! He says all the names. We reach the graveyard in Farmingdale. You sit down and begin to shiver. Everything is all right. These are the holes. The rustle you see they say is a mouse. He shows me the birds. A Blackpoll is a warbler. The feathers on the head are black. This, for instance, is a Broken-Hearted Pinbird. It is hard—that is a tree or a cow or a man out there. On the train they say Mother is lovely. She kisses me hard on the cheek. Mother had the croup when she was a girl. (Mother had a girl.) In history: The boy was born! He goes East and through. Oh, the train ride home! In the station the curtain tugs and you can see the curve in the nub. The man is standing next to the woman. Her mouth closes. The boy kneels. The train brakes. **Q**

Information

Hello—operator? The last town was San Luis. Can you get me Information? The sign says NO GAS.

I do not see anyone. Fifty cents? Here goes. I see snow-capped peaks from here. Can you hear me now? Does the snow stay all year long? The car was running good. I have got more change right here. The place is boarded up. How far is it to the peaks? I drive from dawn to dark. We dial 411 back home. I carry traveler's checks. A car went by. Those peaks look closer. The phone book is gone. Are there any Blanchards listed? They did not slow down. The first name is William. Do you live near the peaks? Here—two quarters and a dime. It is William E. There is not a car in sight. Would you check again? Can you charge my number? Do they climb up to the snow? My last name is Blanchard, too. Gunnison is nice. There are Blanchards in Del Norte, but not one is him. Is there gas in Antonito? My son likes to climb. Is my time up? Just a moment. He is not in Creede. Are the peaks beyond them higher? My change is all gone.

Could you get me Long Distance?

Operator? Are you there? **Q**

A Crucifixion

Our Calvary was a pile of gravel left from the home improvement on the patchy St. Augustine gone to seed and sticker burrs after a hot summer. We made my sister carry a scrap-board cross down the side yard, whipping her when she fell, with branches from the jasmine bushes. It was pretentious of her to think she was the Messiah; she was a girl and only eleven. We had put a crown of real thorns on her head. Up on the hill, wearing a pink one-piece swimming suit, her arms tied to plywood, she uttered her last words: "Oh God, why hast thou forsaken me!" and screamed. A mockingbird shot out of the live oak and the cicadas fell silent. Then Mom came out on the porch and said it was time for lunch. Around the oilcloth, with Kool-Aid moustaches, we spread the French's and the Hunt's, and I gobbled my red wiener, hoping maybe I'd get crucified next. Q

Gates of God

All night we
speak in tongues—
elations of the spread
earth, my tall
tower inside you.

Joseph

You let a ghost fuck you,
but not me, Mary.
The bald slope of your belly
hiding the sweet crack
through which only gods can pass,
headfirst.

Haiku: Safe Sex

The slub of your tongue
flush against my loosened seam—
I will try not to fart.

Family Romance

Oh, Mom, you were the best I ever had.
Freud never understood my story.
It was not the wet breasts I wanted
but the deep reaches of your loins,
where I was in so far
we shuddered together for hours.

Then, when I came
out, all limp and glistening, I spurted
my gold to sting you, Mother,
but you sealed my cock away in your white
    bandage.

Emily Dickinson

You wait so long to walk down
the black river of yourself.
You want to be unfamiliar.

You sit in a chair
of your bones,
the white rose of a handkerchief
pressed against your face.

Your shadow runs a race with itself.
Already it is tomorrow.
Already yesterday.

Shoes

Take note:
you are walking
to your grave.

You will notice at the shore
the many little coffins
tossed in the sand
while the dead wade for hours,

and in the evening how exquisitely
coffins glide across
the ballroom. How polished they are,
reflecting the chandeliers.

You will notice the trails of coffins
across new snow, the open coffins
beside the bed, the poem resting
in the coffins of its strict rhythm.

Many sunny days you will see
more dead than ever. They walk
hand in hand under the elms,
wearing their future: eyes, tongue, sole, lace.

The Water Gatherer

Sometimes my prayers go unanswered.
But if smoke always listened,
why would I pray?

I walk many miles over sand,
riding my shadow like the snake.
During proper visions,

I stop to make offerings,
but my medicine bag grows thin
like a sin that is forgotten.

The lake woman does not need
my ashes. A spider does not
need bones.

After the eighteenth sun,
my spirit climbs the dead tree;
the branches are arrows
shot end to end,
making a ladder to the sky.

Somewhere in the invisible lake,
she laughs. She will sleep,
hiding under her mirror,
knowing I cannot steal her blood.

Easter Sunday

The bell choir hurls its hymn of stones;
one late cue and everything stumbles
into heaven: He is Risen,
and they sit. It is all we can do
to contain ourselves, our cruel relief.

Children move down the doting aisle,
greedy for eggs. The pastor opens
the hasp on his large-lettered book and feeds
each holy cherry into their ears.
He knows they are a tough crowd.

They would writhe out of their skin
into summer. Even the white scattering
of widows will not be still:
they shrink into their bodies,
smiling; all children look like theirs.

A fanfare stirs the lake of hymnals:
everyone stands, and the great slur of praise goes
    out.
The pastor reddens as he sings, wild,
famished, biting into the word God.
And then the pouring of the wine.

Cemetery

The earth wounded
by flowers. Nothing
heals. Not birds
singing nor insects
underground.
There is a hunger
we cannot feed,
a mouth that will
not rest until
it sucks the marrow
from our bones.

Aaron's Rod

We have no honor, save
the bodies that we give
away. A mother smiles
and a child feels exposed.
The boys who undress
in the basement of a church
beat it. At least that.

The Crisis

Sometimes the dog was mistaken
for a man we could not rescue
in time. The postman comes
and goes, leaving an invitation
to a funeral we would rather not
attend, our children stricken
with a host of vermin.

Here I am again in Mamie's shop in Blackwater. I expect it will be the last time I ever write a letter from here. Jim and I are to get hitched on July 5th over at Peninsula Church. I came up early from San Antonio to St. Louis to go shopping for a dress. I found a flouncy one, and a dual-control flag kite for a wedding present for Jim, and a hat for me. My cousin Beverly fixed up the hat. It started out as a little white hat, a kind of Baptist hat, but Beverly put on a ribbon and a flower and a veil, and now I could sail away to Tennessee in a high wind. Then I came on to Blackwater. We are putting all Jim's Texas people up in the town of Arrow Rock, fifteen minutes away. It's now a historical state-preserved town that's so authentic they made two Tom Sawyer movies over there. I remember Arrow Rock when most of the buildings in it were barely standing up. I remember going over there in the winter one time, and looking in the dusty window of the abandoned general store, and seeing a cardboard box full of human bones and a skull. I have no idea what they were doing there. Now it's a tourist attraction, with live theater and craft shows and bed-and-breakfast places, which is where the Texans are going; Jim's mother and sister and his son and daughter and daughter-in-law and grandkids. I got them Texas flags to put up in front of the bed-and-breakfast houses that they are in. Jim is driving up tonight from San Antonio and should be in Oklahoma by now. My cousin is marrying us—Donald McGeehee. He sent me about three different marriage services in a package here to Aunt Mamie's to choose from, so I have been sitting out here in Mamie's shop, typing up my marriage service on this same old manual that I wrote that letter on three years ago, now I think, or maybe it was four. The Episcopalian one is really *stout*—all kinds of thees and thous and trothings at the mouth, like get this: "I require and charge you both, as ye will answer in the dreadful Day of Judgment, when the secrets of the heart shall be disclosed (Why not now? Why wait?) that if either of you knows any impediment. . . ." Something tells me it should be "if either of you-all know any impediment." The other services are a lot looser, but I love that old language—it's like dressing up. So I have put three different versions together. I have dispensed with the Dreadful Day of Judgment and kept other bits; and at the end, Dr. Donald McGeehee, in his awful majesty, pronounces: "By the authority vested in me by the church and the State of Missouri. . . ." I like that bit. There's no air conditioning in that church, so I am making it brief. My sister Sunny will stand up for me, and Jim's son will be his best man. Jim Junior just got back from Saudi Arabia in April. Roger is bringing his bluegrass band, so there will be dancing. That old church needs a wedding for once instead of so many funerals. I told you Mamie's husband's, my uncle Lawrence's, store *fell down* right in the middle of the street last year and expired in a pile of bricks and broken timbers? Well, now Lawrence himself is gone. They buried him at Peninsula not two weeks ago. And here's Aunt Mamie coming to my wedding. I am wondering if Jim has got as far as Big Cabin, and whether he found a nice motel, and I miss him. The girls gave me a shower tonight. There were six of them here in Blackwater that played games together for so many years, and then when Mama died, they wouldn't get a sixth person again—they'll only let me or Sunny or Aunt Maxie sit in and make it six. So I went over to Nettie's with Mamie, and they gave me a good many charming presents, and Bonnie gave me back Mama's wooden gingerbread men and said I should have them. They look like the Five Fates, these elderly white-headed women throwing dice on the tabletop. Except Bonnie Rapp isn't elderly. Jesse Morris is the most white-headed. She has a land grant from her husband's family signed by Andrew Jackson. Did you ever wonder what Andrew Jackson's handwriting was like? It's a big square hand, straight up and down, like teeth. There are cracks in the sidewalk on Main Street, and weeds are growing out of them. Jack's store is closed, and Mamie will move out as soon as she has her house sold. She'll move to Springfield to be close to Don and Glen Leroy, her two sons, and their families. So there will be only four left at the dice game. It was a hundred and four today. Bonnie said there was real trouble here last Halloween. Two kids from out-of-town, whose parents had sent them to Blackwater to stay for a while (maybe to straighten them out or something), got into fights with the local kids. Guns were fired in the air, and three carloads of deputy sheriffs were sent. It's midnight and the moon is up. I feel like I am sending out a last report. Big-city race hatreds have come to Blackwater. Weeds on Main Street. Mamie moving away. The number of the Fates down to four. They roll their five big dice. The dice bang across the table. You hope to come up with a straight, but who knows? I just went outside again, and it looks like heavy weather coming from the west. Lightning. Jim has to get here by noon tomorrow so we can get our license. You have to wait three days. You know, it was his kids that were keeping after us to get married; we were like these old hippies going off to live in sin in Mexico, and his son kept saying, "When are you guys going to get married?" What has happened to the younger generation? The weather is going to pass by to the north. Great numbers of family will gather. We'll sign our names on the Cooper County registry, as have all my great-great ancestors going way back in those yellow old books. Don will read from William Wesley King's giant leather-bound Bible. The band will break out into "Dixie Darling." I'll re-member the rattle of those five dice on the tabletop as long as I live, and Nettie saying, "They're hot!" Nettie, Bonnie, Elsie, Jesse, Mamie. I'm honored to sit in and make up the sixth. **Q**

K ZOO TIRE CO
WHEELS · CUSTOM ACC · SERVICE

Metro 25™
Tire Centers

K ZOO TIRE CO
WHEELS · CUSTOM ACC · SERVICE

SHAVER RD. & CENTRE ST. · 8012 SHAVER RD.
PORTAGE, MI 49002

```
*******************************************************************
*********************************************************************
**                                                               **
**                                                               **
**                                                               **
**          K Z O O   T I R E   C O. / METRO 25                  **
**          ****************************************              **
**                                                               **
**                                                               **
**                   8012 SHAVER ROAD                            **
**                 PORTAGE, MICHIGAN 49002                       **
**                    (616) 327-2587                             **
**                                                               **
**   EMPLOYEE NAME:   JOHN  RYBICKI_____             **
**                                                               **
**   CHECK NUMBER:  1715_____   DATE OF CHECK:  6/13/91_        **
**                                                               **
**   PAY PERIOD STARTING:  6/9/91_____   ENDING:  6/15/91_      **
**                                               25.8            **
**   TOTAL HOURS WORKED THIS WEEK: ___28.5 HRS  20+5.8           **
**                                                               **
**                                                               **
**   GROSS PAY:  ___167.70_____    410.70  150595                **
**   F.I.C.A.:  ___10.40_____      25.4T   9338                  **
**   MEDI-CARE:  ___2.43____       5.96    2186                  **
**   STATE TAX:  ___5.20____       14.56   5396                  **
**   FED TAX:  ___18.00_____       42.00   17300                 **
**   MISC. DEDUCT: ___-0-_____                                  **
**   NET PAY:  ___137.63____                                     **
**                                                               **
**   David Foley                                                 **
**   PREPARED BY:              *    RECEIVED BY:                 **
*********************************************************************
*******************************************************************
```

"SERVING THE NATION"

We feel an affinity with a certain thinker because we agree with him; or because he shows us what we were already thinking; or because he shows us in a more articulate form what we were already thinking; or because he shows us what we were on the point of thinking; or what we would sooner or later have thought; or what we would have thought much later if we hadn't read it now; or what we would have been likely to think but never would have thought if we hadn't read it now; or what we would have liked to think but never would have thought if we hadn't read it now. **Q**

Dear Mr. Rader:

I'm afraid I must count myself among those Jews who annoy you so seriously that they cause you to have a mini-tantrum and get all red in the face right there on color TV. Well, you have a point about us annoying Jews. When annoying Jews like me hear genuinely recognizable Israel-bashing we call it by its right name. Worse yet, when it comes to memorializing the murdered Six Million, we never seem to shut up; you are certainly right about that.

"Criticism of Israel" is something the tumultuously democratic Knesset specializes in, with a lot more vigor (maybe because they've got Deuteronomy and the Prophets as precedents, and right around the corner, so to speak) than Dotson Rader and his friends. And criticism of Israel is easily distinguished from displays not merely of misinformation but of malicious *dis*information, especially in the company of the professionally mendacious media-mongering Dr. Mehdi. His presence alone separates "criticism of Israel" from what is ordinarily understood as Israel-bashing. (The fine line that is said to be inscribed between anti-Zionism and anti-Semitism is generally set down in invisible ink. If, with the possible gifts of X-Ray vision, you can actually *see* that line, perhaps you will wish to discuss its character in public.)

As for your extreme impatience with the way the Jews keep harping on the Holocaust (ah, what a greedy, selfish bunch, those Jews, wanting to keep all that wonderful suffering for themselves!), decade after decade ... well, what is your opinion of the Christians, who keep carrying on and carrying *ON* about the Crucifixion, century after tedious century, even after all the *other* suffering that's been going in in the world? My God, how those Christians keep harping on the Crucifixion! When will they EVER cut it out?

Sincerely,

Cynthia Ozick

Cynthia Ozick

P.S. I forgot to say that since I and the other annoying Jews control the media and all that, and also in view of that Powerful Jewish Lobby in Washington, I admit it's awfully picayune for me to resort to just an ordinary letter to a TV talk show host. Please chalk it up to modesty.

I am glad the book is floundering along through copyeditors and typesetters, despite my unwitting attempts to bring Knopf to its knees and bankruptcy by retyping pages. I will never live it down, never. It will be chipped into my gravestone, SHE RETYPED TEXT AND SO SHE DIED. But I have decided there are big things and small things in life, and the small things I have assigned to an ever-mindful God or Godette, as the case may be, as they are the hardest to deal with, seeing as how they arrive on a daily basis. Big things are for humans: wars, tornadoes, famines, situations in which small people rise to great events (tiny mothers lift cars off children), etc. I have been trying to let the small things go. For instance, Jim is sitting in there in front of his computer, whistling "Delta Dawn." He has been whistling "Delta Dawn" for several weeks now, and I am about to go mad. But instead of going in there and grabbing myself by the throat and falling down and going Arrrgggghhh, etc., I will just let it go. Someday in the future, with no help from me, Jim will quit whistling "Delta Dawn." I don't know what he's doing at the computer. We went to Padre Island with his grandchildren. Evidently, the Daughter Wars are over for the present. His oldest daughter helped throw him a birthday party (the Big Sixty), and then sent his two granddaughters off with us to Padre. His daughter married a Hispanic guy named Aredondo, who works for IBM, and they live in a lovely sort of semi-hippie ranch out at Cedar Creek, near Austin. Padre Island is always foamy with wind and white, floury sand, but we set up tents and windbreaks and had a good time. There are great oil platforms only half a mile offshore. They have this lonely, bell-like whistle that sounds all night over the waves, and the beaches are spotted with tar. At the Buy Your Seashells And T-Shirts Here shops, they sell little packets of Tar Off. Also, farther down the island, we saw an enormous amount of garbage that had floated up from Mexico. I used to get so mad at the condition of Mexican beaches, which were beautiful stretches of pure white sand and coconut groves with slimy plastic waste all over them. And now here the shit is *up here.* A woman told me that the Texas Parks Department had kept people off beaches for three days last week because of medical waste—like syringes—that had been found floating in from Mexico. Then, as we drove south down the beach on Padre, on the other side of Corpus Christi, I started seeing the tell-tale colors of plastic jugs, bottles, and things and stuff, and I told Jim to stop so I could go look at it. Sure enough, there were the familiar yellow plastic bottles marked LIQUIDO PARA FRENOS, brake fluid; and BLANQUEADOR, bleach; strange headless dolls; and those medical bottles with rubber stops that you put a syringe through. That is medical waste, and if there are bottles, somewhere in all that litter there are syringes. And here is cholera creeping up the hemisphere. How is this stuff ending up on the beaches of Padre Island? And *all* of it was Mexican; there wasn't anything marked with English. Jim is also pissed off; he remembers Padre in the early fifties, when it was pristine and he courted girls out on the windswept dunes. He said there wasn't even driftwood then. He said one time he had driven out there with a girl and they were making out on the dunes when they saw two cars driving down the beach from opposite directions, the only two cars on miles and miles of beach. And sure enough, they ran head-on right into each other. Evidently, both drivers were drunk. The heat here has been very, very heavy. It's been over 100 for days. We don't have any air conditioning in this house, but there are attic fans which, when both of them are turned on, will suck you right out of your chair if you don't hang on. But at least it's a breeze. These people we are housesitting for are academics who have framed posters, Oriental rugs, large weighty books of Hieronymus Bosch's paintings (which I like looking at for all the strange, glistening, slender, evil things that are going on in them), and a cat. We had fun with the granddaughters; we let them do anything they wanted, like eat ham sandwiches and soda for breakfast. Next time, we'll take them to San Fernando Cathedral. Jim's first wife (who was these girls' grandmother that they never knew) had a distant ancestor named Luisa Leal, and the Leals were the first Spanish settlers of San Antonio. The Old Man, a great-grandfather ten times removed, is buried under the floor of the old cathedral. Also buried in there are Jim Bowie and Davy Crockett (this will thrill them out of their pigtails). There has been a crime epidemic here in San Antonio; gangs are shooting each other downtown. Lord, Lord, here we are. **Q**

THE LONDON THEY NEVER TELL YOU ABOUT

Wayne Hogan

ANATOMY OF A
TOTAL EXPERIENCE

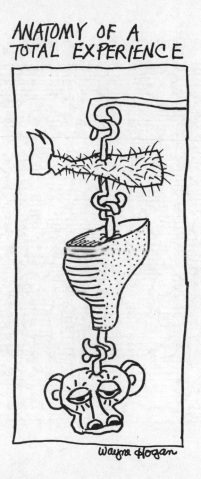

THE INFRASTRUCTURE OF MEDIEVAL SPAIN

ENTERING THE VALLEY OF THE BUTTON-DOWN

CRITIQUE OF PURE CUBISM

RESIDENT POET

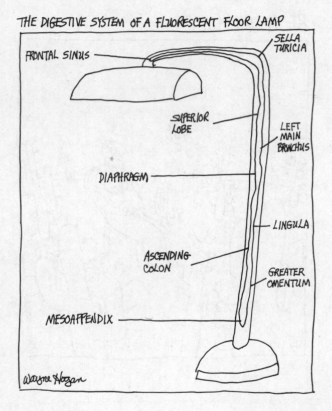

THE DIGESTIVE SYSTEM OF A FLUORESCENT FLOOR LAMP

HANDMADE; ONE-IN-A-MILLION

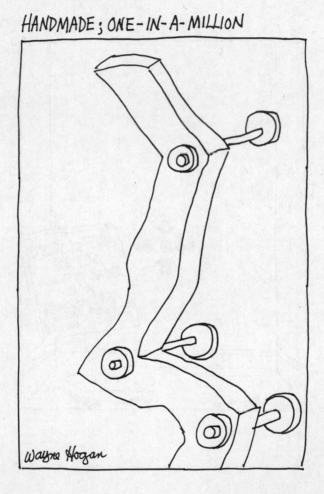

Wayne Hogan

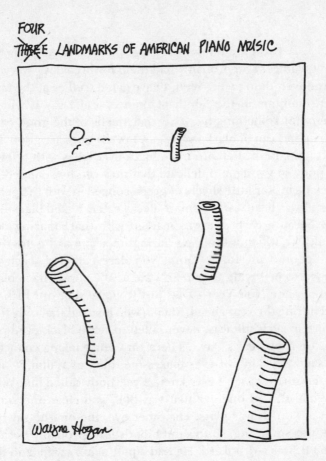

Bet you are one of those people who make a big fuss about truffles. You probably had them for breakfast every day at Andover, didn't you? Well, I have eaten truffles at the fanciest restaurants in the South of France, and I say if you are hungry for something heavenly that smells of the good earth, then open a can of black-eyed peas. Frozen ones are good, too. Of course, best of all are fresh black-eyed peas with a few of the pods so young and delicate that they can be snapped like green beans for little slivers of green cooked in with the pearls. When I was little, I was a smart-alecky eater. I liked black-eyed peas because each one was marked with that amazing deep purple eye which was always gazing up at me as I gathered a pea up onto my fork. "Don't you dare eat me," each pea seemed to be saying to me. So I ate it. We always have black-eyed peas on New Year's Day, just to make sure our luck will hold during the year ahead. Mama, who insisted that only fools believe in such silliness, never failed to serve black-eyed peas to us on New Year's Day. "There's no sense taking chances," she said. Speaking of eyes makes me think of Willie B., who was the sorriest man I ever knew. Everybody called him Willie B. Willie B. had one eye that was blue and clear and stared right at you. It was glass. His other eye, the one he saw you with, was squinting, shifty, and bloodshot—probably because Willie B. was a drunkard. He had a pale skinny wife, and they had an even paler and skinnier little girl. Papa felt sorry for the mess of them and let them move into the house out on the ranch. In exchange, Willie B. was supposed to look after our horses, Charlie and Redwing, and ride fence to make sure the cattle were all right. First thing, Willie B. took one of Papa's calves, sold it, and disappeared over into Menard County. The man who bought the calf told Papa, so Papa was waiting at the ranch when Willie B. finally ran out of whiskey money and showed up on Charlie. Charlie looked all worn out. I could tell Papa was upset, because his voice was shaking. He told Willie B. he'd have to go pack up his wife and little girl and leave. Willie B.'s glass eye was calm and serene, but the bloodshot one looked to me as if it wanted to kill Papa. I think if Willie B. had had a gun, he would have shot us both right there at the barn lot. With Willie B. gone, there was nobody to look after the livestock on the ranch, so Papa said he'd have to sell everything. I said I wanted to keep Redwing because she was the smartest quarter horse I'd ever seen. Redwing could control a whole herd of cattle with me just sitting on her back not knowing a thing but how to hold on to the saddle horn so I wouldn't fall off when she made a sudden shift in direction. Papa said we'd have to keep her closer to town, so I said I'd ride her in the thirteen miles. Well, Redwing had never been off the ranch. We had to go along the highway, and she shied at every automobile, bolting up toward the fences and cutting my legs on the barbed wire. Then she wouldn't cross any bridge. The moment her front hoof made a hollow sound, she reared back, and I'd have to get off and lead her down through every dry ditch and dirty creek between Lohn and Brady. We didn't get home until dark, and Mama was on the front porch wringing her hands because she always thought I didn't have good sense when it came to animals. I never rode Redwing or any other horse again, except once in Central Park when I was trying to impress a girl who was horse-crazy. I switched to bicycles. I got my latest one at Sears Roebuck where I told the salesman, "I want a real bicycle that stops when I reverse the pedals." He said, "You mean a coaster bike?" I did. He ordered a bike like the one I had when I was going to Brady Junior High and had to pump up the only hill in West Texas every morning. I coasted home in the afternoon. I am not a trendy cyclist. I do not have a helmet. I do not have tight black pants that glorify my beautiful backside. I wear old clothes, and I ride around over in Scarsdale where the rich people live.

I look at their superb lawns and golden trees and think how happy they are to be so rich. As I pass by, I hear people say, "Did you see that old fart on that red bike? He has no gears!" My bike says Huffy on it. Can you imagine? Hey, that's the nickname of a sister-in-law of mine. She's married to Emisa, my little brother. They live in Austin. People think that Emisa and my brother Gaddis have odd names. But I was reading a history of the early days in Texas, and I noted some names that people there gave to their children. What do you think of these, son? Alvis, Agnese, Escrage, Mirabeau, Ashbel, Ima, Orissa, Oveta, Heziah, Lillo, Justina, Juylan, Rienzi, Naurice, and Daffan. Damn, I love Texas! **Q**

FOR CREDIT-CARD ORDERS OF BACK NUMBERS, CALL TOLL-FREE,
AT 1-800-733-3000. PRICES AND ISBN CODES SHOWN BELOW.
OR PURCHASE BY CHECK OR MONEY ORDER VIA LETTER TO
SUBSCRIPTION OFFICE. NOTE ADDITION OF POSTAGE AND
HANDLING CHARGE AT $1.50 THE COPY PER EACH COPY REQUESTED.

Q1	$6.95	394-74697-x	Q11	$7.95	679-72173-8
Q2	$5.95	394-74698-8	Q12	$7.95	679-72153-3
Q3	$5.95	394-75536-7	Q13	$8.95	679-72743-4
Q4	$5.95	394-75537-5	Q14	$8.95	679-72893-7
Q5	$6.95	394-75718-1	Q15	$9.95	679-73231-4
Q6	$6.95	394-75719-x	Q16	$9.95	679-73244-6
Q7	$6.95	394-75936-2	Q17	$10.00	679-73494-5
Q8	$6.95	394-75937-0	Q18	$10.00	679-73495-3
Q9	$7.95	679-72139-8	Q19	$10.00	679-73690-5
Q10	$7.95	679-72172-x	Q20	$10.00	679-73691-3

Q21 $10.00 679-73691-3